D1372518

Ending
Aid Dependence

Fahamu Books

China's New Role in Africa and the South: A Search for a New Perspective (2008)

Africa's Long Road to Rights: Reflections on the 20th Anniversary of the African Commission on Human and Peoples' Rights (2008)

Long trajet de l'Afrique vers les droits: Réflexions lors du 20ème anniversaire de la Commission Africaine des Droits de l'Homme et des Peuples (2008)

From the Slave Trade to 'Free' Trade: How Trade Undermines Democracy and Justice in Africa (2007)

Silences in NGO Discourse: The Role and Future of NGOs in Africa (2007)

African Perspectives on China in Africa (2007)

Grace, Tenacity and Eloquence: The Struggle for Women's Rights in Africa (2007)

Breathing Life into the African Union Protocol on Women's Rights in Africa (2006)

Vulgarisation du protocole de l'Union Africaine sur les droits des femmes en Afrique (2006)

African Voices on Development and Social Justice: Editorials from Pambazuka News 2004 (2005)

For further details see www.fahamu.org.

South Centre publications

See the complete list in English, French and Spanish at www.southcentre.org.

Ending
Aid Dependence

Yash Tandon

Foreword by
Benjamin W. Mkapa

fahamu
books

Published 2008 by Fahamu – Networks for Social Justice
Cape Town, Dakar, Nairobi and Oxford
www.fahamu.org   www.pambazuka.org

and

South Centre
Geneva
www.southcentre.org

Fahamu, 2nd floor, 51 Cornmarket Street, Oxford OX1 3HA, UK
Fahamu Kenya, PO Box 47158, 00100 GPO, Nairobi, Kenya
Fahamu Senegal, 9 Cité Sonatel 2, POB 25021, Dakar-Fann, Dakar, Senegal
Fahamu South Africa, c/o 27A Esher St, Claremont, 7708,
Cape Town, South Africa

South Centre, CP 228, 1211 Geneva 19, Switzerland

First published 2008
Second edition 2008

British Library Cataloguing in Publication Data

A catalogue record for this book is available from the British Library

ISBN: 978-1-906387-31-0 2nd edition
(ISBN: 978-1-906387-29-7 1st edition)

Manufactured on demand by Lightning Source

Foreword

Benjamin W. Mkapa
President of Tanzania 1995–2005

The primary and long-term objective of this monograph is to initiate a debate on development aid, and to lay out a do-able strategy for ending aid dependence. An exit strategy from aid dependence requires a radical shift both in the mindset and in the development strategy of countries dependent on aid, and a deeper and direct involvement of people in their own development. It also requires a radical and fundamental restructuring of the institutional aid architecture at the global level.

The first edition of the book was published just before the high level meeting in September 2008 in Accra organised by the OECD and the World Bank. The aim then was to caution the developing countries against endorsing the Accra Action Agenda (AAA), which was based on the OECD's Paris Declaration on Aid Effectiveness (PDAE). The PDAE is built on five principles that on first sight look benign. However, on closer analysis, it turns out to be a formula for subjecting aid recipients to a discipline of collective control by the donors right down to the village level, especially in the poorer and more vulnerable countries in Africa, Asia, Latin America and the Caribbean. However, since no serious discussion on the PDAE had taken place in the South, it was not surprising that the AAA was endorsed in Accra by the generally low-level official delegations from the South and several mostly North-dominated intergovernmental organisations. Conspicuously absent, for example, was the African Union. There are fundamental contradictions between the AAA-endorsed Paris Declaration on Aid Effectiveness (PDAE) and the South Centre's strategy on Aid Exit (SCAE). A simple schema (Table 1) at the end of this Foreword illustrates these differences.

The question is: how do we move forward from here? Making aid 'effective' will only serve to perpetuate aid dependence. There has to be a strategy for ending aid dependence. This book suggests for debate and further discussion a seven-step strategy for ending aid dependence. The first step is the most difficult, that of transforming a mindset anchored in aid. It has taken deep roots in the psyche of the people, especially in the poorer countries of the South. It is similar to drug addiction. Any suggestion of withdrawal from the addiction traumatises its user, and sends them into panic; the longer the addiction lasts the more difficult it becomes to escape. Nonetheless, a start has to be made.

Paradoxically, the AAA has come at a time when the developed industrial North is in the midst of a financial meltdown. How can it help the South when its own house is in disorder, when it is itself dependent on sovereign wealth funds from the South? This question was not asked or addressed at Accra. Could it be that aid, or official development assistance, is not a means of aiding the South but a means of aiding the crisis-ridden Northern economies? At a time when the competition for oil, fuels, land and commodities is heating up between the older industrial countries of the North and the emerging industrial countries of the South such as Brazil, China, India and South Africa, 'aid' from the North could be a means of tying down the aid recipient countries – especially in Africa, which appears to be the principal target for aid – to the colonial apron strings of the older empire.

The question that the international community should be asking is not how the North may provide largesse to the South, but how the global financial infrastructure, now in total disarray, might be restructured. This book draws a distinction between reformism and parallelism. Whilst attempts are being made to reform institutions like the World Bank and the International Monetary Fund, it is evident that these post-Second World War behemoths have lost legitimacy and relevance. Efforts must now be made to set up parallel institutions, especially regional ones, to replace these dated and unreformable bodies. Indeed, the demand of the moment is for another Bretton Woods conference, this time in a location in the South, with a view to creating new institutions of global economic governance. These would genuinely work towards the welfare of poor people in the South and be accountable to the entire international community, and not just to that small fraction, the so-called coalition of the willing.

The message of this book needs to be seriously considered and debated by all those that are interested in the development of the countries of the South. If this means the rethinking of old concepts and methods of work, then let it be so.

Table 1 The South Centre's strategy on aid exit in contrast to the Paris Declaration's strategy on aid effectiveness

This table demonstrates the essential difference in approach between the OECD's proposed Paris Declaration on Aid Effectiveness strategy, and the aid exit strategy proposed by the South Centre.

Characteristics	Paris Declaration (aid effectiveness)
Objective or effect	To perpetuate aid dependency
Strategy	Reform the system so it remains in essence the same. It has no direction
Epistemology	Thinking within the box
Development aid	Assumption that aid will result in development
Relation to the United Nations	Outside the UN system
Relation to the World Bank and the IMF	Within the World Bank-IMF system
Relation with civil society or NGOs	Formal but peripheral inclusion, with inputs that make little or no impact on predetermined agenda
Ownership	Remains essentially with the donors and the World Bank
Accountability	'Mutual' accountability – in reality, accountability to donors
Conditionalities	Performance conditionalities as in practice enforced by donors
Compliance	Compliance tests as laid out by donors
Harmonisation	With donor-set objectives, e.g. trade liberalisation, privatisation, etc
Predictabilty	Donor and budget support is inherently unpredictable and unenforceable; the idea itself creates aid dependence

The Paris Declaration's aid effectiveness strategy was initiated by the OECD, the Northern rich countries' think tank, in association with the World Bank. The aid exit strategy is initiated by the South Centre, which is an independent think tank of the South, supported by most of the bigger countries of the South and working closely with the poorer countries, including all African, Caribbean, Pacific and least developing countries.

South Centre (aid exit)

To exit aid dependency

Development of a 7-point strategy to exit aid dependence

Thinking outside the box

Aid can actually undermine development

Within the UN system

Outside the World Bank-IMF system

Southern civil society is the core of strategic thinking; Northern civil society is part of solidarity

Passes on to national democratic forces

Self-accountability within national democratic processes

Democratic conditionality in the evolving democratisation process

Compliance as laid out by peoples' movements – trades unions, peasant organisations, women's movement, civil society

With people-driven objectives – which could include e.g. protection of local industry, agriculture and SMEs

Predictability of national revenue from citizens and domestic economy, as opposed to aid predictability

Acknowledgments

There are far too many to whom I owe a debt, directly or indirectly, for inspiring me to write this book. I am especially grateful to Benjamin W. Mkapa, immediate former President of the United Republic of Tanzania and chairman of the South Centre, for encouraging me think about Ending Aid Dependence, for reading the first draft and agreeing to write the Foreword.

I am also obliged to the following friends, reviewers and readers of the first edition of the book, who drew my attention to its shortcomings and strengths: Armand Rioust de Largentaye, Elvira Groll, Thomas Lines, Bill Morton, Henri Valot, Rasna Warah, Kath Noble, Adu Koranteng and Lucy Hayes. I am also grateful to the following, who put time aside to read the manuscript, in spite of other more pressing demands – Chief Emeka Anyaoku, Helene Bank, Horace Campbell, Irfan Ul Haque, Norman Girvan, Carlos Lopes, Vikas Nath and Vicente Yu. I alone bear responsibility for the weaknesses of the book.

My special thanks go to Vikas Nath and my publishers, Fahamu Books, for their hands-on advice on the art and skills of printing and outreach. Last but not least, I must thank my research assistant, Xuan Zhang, for her helpful suggestions for improving the text, and my wife, Mary, for not only being the first to read the initial, messy draft, but also for sharing every moment of the joy of writing this book.

Yash Tandon
Geneva, September 2008

Contents

Foreword   v

Acknowledgments   x

Abbreviations   xiii

**1 The bigger picture: Why should developing countries
     escape aid dependence?**   1
Is aid what it says it is?   1
OECD's definition of development aid   4
What is development?   12
Aid taxonomy   16
A litany of false questions and solutions   39
Conclusion   41

2 Case histories: the consequences of aid dependence   44
Red Aid – the poisoned chalice   44
Structural adjustment: Zambia 1978–2002   45
Structural adjustment: Zimbabwe 1980–97   47
Other cases   58
Conclusion and postscript   62

3 An exit strategy: seven steps to end aid dependence   65
Introduction   65
The national project   66
What creates aid dependence?   75
Seven steps to end aid dependence   77

**4 The international aid architecture: structures, processes
     and issues**   103
The international aid architecture   103
Restructuring the architecture: parallelism and reform   116

5 Summary and conclusions: the future of aid   128

Index   136

About the author   144

This book is dedicated to all those who dare
to challenge the ruling intellectual orthodoxy that
services the dominant global political order

Abbreviations

AAA	Accra Action Agenda
ACP	African, Caribbean and Pacific
AFRICOM	Africa Command
BRIC countries	Brazil, Russia, India and China
CFU	Commercial Farmers Union (Zimbabwe)
CSOs	civil society organisations
DAC	Development Assistance Committee
DCF	Development Cooperation Forum
EPAs	Economic Partnership Agreements
ESAP	Zimbabwe's 1991 structural adjustment programme
EU	European Union
FDI	foreign direct investment
GDP	gross domestic product
GNI	gross national income
GPGs	global public goods,
IADGs	internationally agreed development goals
IBRD	International Bank for Reconstruction and Development
IGO	international governmental organisation
INGO	international non-governmental organisation
ILO	International Labour Organisation
IMF	International Monetary Fund
ITC	International Trade Centre
LDCs	least developed countries
MDGs	Millennium Development Goals
NAM	Non-Aligned Movement
NAMA	non-agricultural market access
NATO	North Atlantic Treaty Organisation

NEPAD	New Partnership for Africa's Development
NERP	New Economic Recovery Programme (Zambia)
NIEO	New International Economic Order
NIIO	New International Information Order
ODA	official development assistance
OEI	official equity investments
OECD	Organisation for Economic Cooperation and Development
PDAE	Paris Declaration on Aid Effectiveness
PRSPs	Poverty Reduction Strategy Papers
SAP	structural adjustment programme
SDF	Social Development Fund (Zimbabwe)
SDR	special drawing rights
UDI	unilateral declaration of independence
UN	United Nations
UNCTAD	United Nations Conference on Trade and Development
UNDP	United Nations Development Programme
UNECA	United Nations Economic Commission for Africa
UNFCCC	UN Framework Convention on Climate Change
WCO	World Customs Organisation
WIPO	World International Property Organisation
WPAE	the DAC's Working Party on Aid Effectiveness
WTO	World Trade Organisation
ZCTU	Zimbabwe Congress of Trade Unions

CHAPTER 1

THE BIGGER PICTURE
Why should developing countries escape aid dependence?

Is aid what it says it is?

Aid is well recognised as a contributor to global financial flows, and yet it defies description. It sounds positive because in the public eye and the media it is associated with 'development', 'solidarity' and 'humanitarian' causes. But not all aid goes for these causes, and much that passes as developmental or humanitarian may indeed have little legitimate claim to be either.

The matter of 0.7 per cent

The 0.7 per cent pledge has become a promise to chain the aid dependent 'poor' nations to largesse from the rich in perpetuity. This percentage has become such an oft repeated mantra in the development discourse that it has acquired a mystical aura. Governments of the developed countries have pledged to put aside 0.7 per cent of their gross national income (GNI) for 'aid'. Proposed initially by the World Council of Churches in 1958 as 1.0 per cent of GNI, the principle was adopted by the UN in October 1970 and a target of 0.7 per cent was set. For the last 38 years, the 0.7 per cent pledge has ritually occupied at least a few sentences if not whole paragraphs in all major resolutions that are passed in the name of development or economic growth.

In the media and public discourse the 0.7 per cent has become the single most important yardstick for measuring developed countries' commitment to the development of developing countries. For example, the Scandinavian countries score well and are generally regarded as the friendliest developed countries. The biggest single defaulter is the US. In 2006 its official development assistance (ODA) was $22.7 billion, a fall of 20 per cent in real terms, according to the OECD.

However, the developed countries' actions suggest that, barring half a dozen of them, none of them have any serious intention of ever fulfilling their pledge. Nonetheless, even unfulfilled, the promise itself serves a useful political purpose in domestic and international public relations. For the South governments the non-fulfillment of the promise by the North gets them off the hook – they can blame their countries' lack of development on the lack of aid flows from countries of the North. It gives civil society (and the so-called non-government organisations, or NGOs) of both the North and the South something to moan about when the developed countries do not meet the 0.7 per cent target.

As for the governments of the countries in the North that do not keep to their promise, they have two courses open to them – either ignore the moaning and groaning and refuse to be named and shamed, or create phantom aid and make use of creative conceptual and accounting tricks to boost their ODA figures. In fact, they resort to both strategies. Debt relief and swaps, inflated transaction and administrative costs, overvalued technical assistance, politically motivated aid and military aid, domestic costs linked to refugees are all considered as parts of ODA.

So the 0.7 per cent is stuck. The developing countries and civil society will not abandon it lest the developed world is let off the hook, and the developed world (barring half a dozen countries) largely ignores it or resorts to conceptual and accounting tricks to boost it.

Ending aid dependence

Does all this sound too cynical? It is not supposed to. Our aim is to take stock of aid's importance and try and separate the chaff from the wheat. Our aim is to understand what aid is all about, to put it in a proper political and historical context. Above all, our aim, ultimately, is to do away with aid, to exit from it, even if it means letting the developed countries off the hook and obliging developing countries to take charge of their own development.

In other words, despite its positive connotations, aid is not such a good thing after all. The moment you add the word 'dependence' to aid, it loses its lustre. It becomes a millstone round the necks of those that are aid dependent. The 0.7 per cent pledge becomes a promise that ties the aid dependent poor nations to largesse from the rich.

A question of accountability

Some questions need to be asked of the governments of the South that depend on aid. How does an aid dependent African (or any other) government fulfil its pledge to its own people to be democratically accountable if 25 per cent (or in some cases 50 per cent) of its national budget is financed out of donor aid? What kind of 'development' is it encouraging if 75 per cent (in some cases 100 per cent) of the development-kind-of-aid comes from outside the country? When a country claims poverty as a reason for seeking aid from outside, is the country really poor? In the name of aid or capital from the rich countries, does it not undervalue the worth of its own people's intelligence and ingenuity, the labour of its workers and farmers, its young people, the value of its natural resources?

Is the aid-dependent government accountable to its people or to the donors who finance the government? Can citizens be assured that their interests will be safeguarded by their own national governments and not become subservient to controls exerted by donors on their national governments? Can citizens of aid-dependent countries ever escape the stigma where the value of their industriousness and entrepreneurship will always be overshadowed by the value and importance given to aid?

The national project

These and some other questions need to be asked, and a way found to exit aid dependence, placing developing countries on the road to national and regional self-reliance in what this book later describes as 'the national project'. Escaping from aid dependence is an exercise in political economy; it involves trusting a country's own people to bring about development through proper use and management of its own natural resources, the labour of its workers, farmers and entrepreneurs, and its peoples' ingenuity. Development is not (should not be) a matter left to aid, and certainly not something left to the donors. They, it is important to understand, have no obligation to transfer resources into the South without getting something in return when, even in the richest country of all – the US – their own poor need these resources. Indeed, governments in the South should feel embarrassed taking aid from countries like the US where there are long lines of people at soup kitchens for the poor, and where the poor do not have proper access to medical care and where household debt relative to personal disposable income is over 100 per cent. Governments in Africa should not ask for aid from a country like China or India where the poor may well be poorer than the poor in Africa. There are other kinds of more honest relationships that can be encouraged between them, based on trade, investments, technology and tourism, for example, without calling these aid.

This monograph seeks to provide some reflections on how the 'donors' and the 'recipients' might liberate themselves from this aid dependence. Aid exit is good for all. It should be at the top of the political agenda of all countries.

OECD's definition of development aid

The OECD's Development Assistance Committee (DAC) has a complex definition of ODA. On its website it has a guide called 'Is it ODA?'[1] to help donors 'to decide whether a particular expenditure qualifies as ODA', but in the final analysis only the 'DAC may determine such eligibility'. The DAC Statistical Reporting

Directives are designed to help statistical correspondents to complete the DAC questionnaire, supplemented by a *Handbook for Reporting Debt Reorganisation on the DAC Questionnaire*. These provide definitions and detailed descriptions of the concepts and categories used in the DAC statistics.[2]

The decisive criteria for determining ODA eligibility

According to the DAC:

Official development assistance is defined as those flows to countries on the DAC List and to multilateral institutions for flows to ODA recipients which are:

i. Provided by official agencies, including state and local governments, or by their executive agencies; and

ii. Each transaction which:

a) is administered with the promotion of the economic development and welfare of developing countries as its main objective; and

b) is concessional in character and conveys a grant element of at least 25 per cent (calculated at a rate of discount of 10 per cent).[3]

On how the 25 per cent concessional aspect of loans was arrived at, the directive explains:

From the earliest discussions of the concept of ODA, Members agreed that it should represent some effort in favour of developing countries by the official sector. Loans at market terms were excluded. When, in the early 1970s, interest rates began rising sharply, it was further specified that loans could only be reported as ODA if they had a grant element of at least 25 per cent, calculated against a notional reference rate of 10 per cent per annum.

These elements remain today. In recent years, long-term interest rates in most OECD Member countries have fallen well below 10 per cent, so the 25 per cent grant element level has become easier to attain. But to qualify as ODA, loans

must still be concessional in character, i.e. below market interest rates.[4]

In other words, the burden of a 25 per cent concessional loan is much less than it was when it was first set.

As the directive says: 'This is often the decisive criterion for determining ODA eligibility. In the final analysis *it is a matter of intention* [emphasis added]'.[5] But in order to reduce the scope for subjective interpretations and promote comparable reporting, members have agreed to include, for example, the following within the ODA definition:

- Assistance to refugees
- Costs of secondary and tertiary education provided to developing country nationals in the donor country
- Administrative costs of ODA programmes
- Programmes to raise development awareness in donor countries
- Official equity investments in a developing country (reported as ODA because of their development intention).

On the other hand, the following are excluded from being counted as ODA, for example:

- Military aid
- Enforcement aspects of peacekeeping
- Paramilitary functions of police work
- Military use of nuclear energy.

Annex 2 of the Statistical Reporting Directives[6] lists those contributions from international agencies which are reportable as ODA. The directives also list the main international non-governmental organisations' (INGOs) contributions that are reportable as ODA. These are increasingly numerous. Where members have contributed to INGOs not on the list, they are asked to assess their ODA character in the light of the INGOs' aims, programmes and membership. If they believe the contribution should be counted as ODA, they are asked to inform the secretariat so that members can consider the INGO in the annual review.

The directive defines 'flows' as:

> transfers of resources, either in cash or in the form of commodities or services. ... Repayments of the principal of ODA loans count as negative flows, and are deducted to arrive at net ODA, so that by the time a loan is repaid, the net flow over the period of the loan is zero. Interest is recorded, but is not counted in the net flow statistics. Where official equity investments in a developing country are reported as ODA because of their development intention, proceeds from their later sale are recorded as negative flows, regardless of whether the purchaser is in a developed or a developing country.[7]

However:

> Capital investment in the donor country is not regarded as a flow and is therefore not eligible to be reported as ODA. This applies even to the construction and equipment of training and research facilities related to development issues. The running costs of such facilities may, however, be counted as ODA.[8]

This, then, is the summary of DAC's definition of development aid. It has become ingrained as part of the received orthodoxy on aid, part of the prevailing wisdom, the norm. It has become an axiomatic definition on aid. Barring a few independent thinkers and NGOs, the DAC definitions and methodology have not been subjected to serious and critical analysis, particularly by the recipient countries.

Conceptual, statistical and operational flaws

The most difficult problem in critiquing the OECD-DAC definition of what constitutes ODA is that it is now conventionalised as *the* standard definition of ODA. It has acquired, as it were, a prescriptive legitimacy. Based on this, statistics on 'development aid' are collected by the DAC and quoted world-wide by the mushrooming aid industry *literati* – including inter-governmental organisations (for example, the World Bank, the IMF, the Economic Commission for Africa, the African Union); national governments (including recipient countries); and otherwise independent experts, scholars, researchers and writers. Every use of those statistics gives (spurious) legitimacy to both the veracity of the statistics and distorts the very notion of development.

Leaving aside the definition of development, to which we shall come later, giving a precise definition to the elusive concept of aid must indeed be very difficult. How much more difficult must it be for donors and for the DAC to give these definitions operational function and numeric values. Let us pose a few questions.

Why should military aid be *a priori* excluded from ODA? The reason for it is supposed to be axiomatic, perhaps commonsensical. But is it really that simple? (See '3 Yellow Aid – military and political aid', later in this chapter for a discussion on this.)

The administrative costs of ODA programmes are part of ODA, including presumably, costs incurred in the donor countries themselves. What precisely are these 'administrative costs', and how are they calculated and who benefits from them?

Programmes to raise development awareness in donor countries are part of ODA. These are monies spent within the donor countries. Why should the recipient developing countries pay for them? And in any case, on whose definition of development is such awareness created? Among whom?

Indeed, even when development experts and consultants come, for example, to Africa from the donor countries to advise African governments on development and have their costs counted as ODA to be paid back to the donor countries, are these consultants serving recipient or donor country interests? Did developing countries express an interest in receiving such paid advice? Furthermore, where do the experts pay their tax and value added on their services?

The 25 per cent concessionary aid is of questionable value, when interest rates are falling. And yet it is regarded as the touchstone of ODA loans. What then happens to the remaining 75 per cent of the loan? This eventually has to be paid back, of course. What is the effect of this on the debt burden of the recipient countries that have been lured to accept the whole loan because of its concessional content? What is revealed about the concessional loans by the donors may seem alluring but what is hidden may be damaging to the recipient countries in the long run.

Much of the aid is tied to procurement from the donors. According to the UN, tying of aid to purchasing of goods and services increases costs by 25 to 60 per cent.[9] In other words, the real value of their ODA must be reduced by a quarter or more. This wipes out any concessionary 25 per cent content of the loans. How legitimate is it to still classify it as aid?

Some of the ODA takes the form of making communities in the donor countries aware of their development obligations. But why is this considered as part of ODA? Furthermore, when donors allocate such funds to awareness-raising activities in their own countries, is there a mechanism by which the recipients are consulted about the usefulness of this exercise?

Also vast amounts of money are injected into institutions such as the World Bank, the United Nations Conference on Trade and Development (UNCTAD) and the World Trade Organisation (WTO) by donor governments and their development agencies to argue the case for foreign direct investments (FDIs), and trade and financial liberalisation, and to persuade the developing countries to open up their doors to FDIs for their own good through expensive seminars and workshops. In reality, FDIs bring profits to the rich corporations, and their local agents in the recipient countries. One-sided and biased calculations of presumed benefits in terms of employment, technology transfer, transfer of know-how, etc are seldom set against costs incurred. Existing empirical evidence generates serious doubt about how much good they do to the poor in developing countries. So the developing countries are paying twice for this privilege – first for the seminars and work-shops, and second when donor-based corporations take profits out of the FDI-receiving countries.

The official equity investments (OEIs) by developed country donor agencies in a developing country are reported as ODA 'because of their development intention'. The first question is: Has anybody done research into what these OEIs are and whose interest they really serve? Secondly, does equity (whether private or official) acquire a developmental character simply by the intention of the investors?

The DAC statistics capture only the inflows of funds from the North to the South, based on fairly complex measures and computations, which are little understood and have largely remained unchanged over time. However, a similar conceptual or computational model does not exist to calculate outflows from the developing to the developed countries. By some reckoning these amounts are far more than the inflows. There is, in other words, a reverse flow from the South to the North. Who, then, is aiding whom?

The DAC is its own collective judge and jury. The DAC peer reviews each member country's policies and performance about once every four years, based on statistics provided by individual donor countries, and on the simple equation that ODA flows = growth = development. As long as the donor countries follow the definition of ODA, they are deemed to have satisfied the description of development aid. There is no outside independent body with operational capacity or proper conceptual tools to vouch for the accuracy of the figures or collective self-evaluations done by this club of donors.

These questions can be multiplied several times over. In the light of these problems with ODA, conceptually and operationally, the following statements, for example, raise some questions that need to be addressed.

- At the 2005 G8 Gleneagles meeting, the 15 largest EU aid donors committed themselves to reach the 0.7 per cent of gross national income target by 2015, and 0.56 per cent by 2010.[10] On this basis, in mid-2005, the OECD judged that by 2010 ODA would increase by $50 billion, including an additional $25 billion for Africa. Of course, other than themselves, there is nobody to monitor whether the 15 donors deliver what they promised, or whether it is new aid money or simply movement of money from one aid envelope to another. Also, what do these figures mean in real terms, except as a general non-enforceable promissory note?

- The Blair Commission for Africa[11] called for a doubling of aid to sub-Saharan Africa by 2010, from $25 billion to $50 billion a year, with a further increase to $75 billion by 2015, which the commission added, 'would be well within the target of 0.7 per cent of GNI for aggregate ODA'.[12] There is no mechanism to monitor, let alone evaluate, whether this actually happens, and whether in fact these figures represent real value.

- 'By the early 1990s, 75 per cent of British food aid was channelled through NGOs, 40 per cent of Swedish emergency spending through Swedish NGOs and the figures for the United States (excluding food aid) had risen to 65 per cent by mid-1990s.'[13] What do these figures really mean? Also, emergency food aid, while necessary in certain circumstances, can be counter productive if the fundamental issues that created the emergency are not addressed.

Conclusion

- First, there is no question that the OECD-DAC definitions of development and of aid have serious problems. There is urgent need to define development from the developing countries' rather than donor point of view. In any case, the formula that says that ODA flows = growth = development is so simplistic and one-

dimensional that it is surprising that few independent
writers on aid, in both the South as well as the North,
have dived deeper than these shallow intellectual waters
of the DAC.

- Second, the DAC definitions and statistics on
  development aid cannot be relied upon as even
  proximate estimates of real flows. These are vastly
  exaggerated in DAC ODA figures and may, indeed, be
  seen as a cover up for what, in reality, are reverse flows
  from the South to the North.
- Third, there is also need for a new taxonomy of
  development aid that is more realistic and measurable
  from the developing countries' point of view, rather
  than one based on the DAC's one-basket concept. We
  need a taxonomy that captures the conceptual and
  operational complexity of development aid.

Suggested below are a definition of development and a fresh taxonomy of development aid from a Southern perspective.

What is development?

In contrast to the OECD-DAC's delivery concept of development
as an act that pours money and technical assistance into recipients
that are assumed not be able to think, act, plan or implement for
themselves, without being monitored and evaluated by the donors,
we argue that development has essentially two components:

1 Development is self-defined; it cannot be defined by
  outsiders. Within the national framework, it is defined
  in an evolving democratic process as part of the national
  project (explained later). In this long evolutionary
  development process, decision making and control over
  national resources pass into the hands of the population
  and their democratic institutions.

2 Development is a process of self-empowerment. As the
  struggle for gender equality, for example, teaches us,

development is a long process of struggle for liberation from structures of domination and control, including mental constructs and the use of language. This struggle is waged between nations, within nations, within communities, and even within households.

A more detailed discussion of these concepts is to be found in various writings (from 1963 to 1999) of the late Mwalimu Julius Nyerere, the first president of Tanzania and the founding spirit behind the South Centre. These are some of his ideas on the subject:

- Development is a process; it starts from within the individual, communities and the nation.
- It is the realisation of the potential for self-support and contributing to society.
- It involves the building of self-confidence.
- It aims at leading lives of dignity, which include gainful employment that helps individuals to meet basic needs, security, equity and participation. These lead to self-fulfilment.
- It is freedom from fear of want and exploitation.
- It is freedom from political, economic and social exploitation.
- It is the continuous struggle for the right and access to decision making that affects the life and livelihood of the individual, the community, the nation and the region.

These ideas form the ideological glue of development. Borrowing from Nyerere, and against the background of the struggle for emancipation from colonial and imperial economic exploitation and national oppression, development from a Southern perspective may be defined by means of the following formula:

$$Development = SF + DF - IF$$

where:

- SF is the social factor – the essential well-being of the

people free from want and exploitation
- DF is the democratic factor – the right of the people to participate in decision making that affects their lives and livelihoods
- IF is the imperial factor – the right of a nation to liberation from colonial and imperial domination, which follows from the right to self-determination.

Imperialism is often a taboo word, usually avoided in polite intellectual discourse. But here we mean no more than what the London *Financial Times* of 13 May 2008 said in its editorial, 'Food investment, not imperialism'. Having advocated foreign investments as a solution to the problem of food crisis, it went on to say:

> The only exception is if investment in agriculture turns into imperialism. That is a practice with a long and unpleasant history, from the plantation agriculture of the European empires to the 1954 coup in Guatemala, assisted by the US Central Intelligence Agency, at least in part for the benefit of the United Fruit Company.[14]

How, then, do we define development from a Southern perspective?

> Development, in its most inclusive sense, means the satisfaction of the basic material and social needs of the people (especially those most vulnerable) through a system of governance that is democratic and accountable to the people, and through minimising (and if possible eliminating) imperial interventions in developing societies.

This definition is a far cry from the neoliberal donor formula for development, to wit:

$$Development = Growth + Wealth\ accumulation$$

where:

- Growth = open markets + foreign investments + good governance (as defined by developed country donors

and the multilateral agencies that they control)
- Wealth accumulation = ensuring that the rich continue to get richer and are able to amass fortunes, with trickle-down effect of some of the benefits to the poor.

The *Growth Report: Strategies for Sustained Growth and Inclusive Development* of the World Bank initiated Commission on Growth and Development, 2008,[15] has an even shallower definition of 'growth', and no discussion of how growth leads to 'inclusive development'. After examining 13 'success stories' (Botswana, Brazil, China, Hong King China, Indonesia, Japan, Republic of Korea, Malaysia, Malta, Oman, Singapore, Taiwan (China) and Thailand), the report identified the following five 'striking points of resemblance'[16] between them:

- They fully exploited the world economy.
- They maintained macroeconomic stability.
- They mustered high rates of savings and investment.
- They let markets allocate resources.
- They had committed, credible and capable governments.

Besides being incredibly shallow conceptually, these five 'striking points' are meaningless generalisations and, in some cases, a complete travesty of reality.

It is fair to add, however, that the donor countries that follow the social democratic model have a variation of the growth model in their own countries, expressed, in simple terms, as the following:

Development = Open markets + Investments + Good governance
+ Redistribution

where Redistribution = Taxing the rich to give to the poor. As donors, the social democratic countries hope or expect that their model is replicable in the recipient countries. But where this formula is exported to the developing recipient countries, it often becomes a grotesque caricature of the 'pure' model. The following is a simple expression of this:

Growth = Open markets + Foreign investments + Good governance
(as defined by the donors and the multilateral agencies that they
control)

Wealth accumulation = Ensuring that the rich continue to get
richer and amass fortunes

Redistribution = Taxing the rich to give to the poor
(usually taxing the less poor and the middle classes, for the rich
employ lawyers and accountants to hide their wealth and outwit
the tax collector)

The formula from the Southern perspective (Development = SF + DF − IF) is not only national, but also regional and even continental. It is also the basis for expanding it to South–South cooperation. Here too, Nyerere made a unique contribution. He was not only a great nationalist leader, but also a visionary Pan-African and third world leader. In the 1980s, he chaired the South Commission set up by the developing countries. The political rationale and teleological direction of the South Commission Report was succinctly summarised by Nyerere in these five headings:

- Development shall be people centred
- Pursue a policy of maximum national self-reliance
- Supplement that with a policy of maximum collective South–South self-reliance
- Build maximum South–South solidarity in your relations with the North
- Develop science and technology.

Aid taxonomy

All science begins with classification, a taxonomy. Oranges and bananas may have certain qualities in common (some vitamins for example), but it is important to understand each fruit separately when growing and eating them. In the aid industry everything is often jumbled up in a single basket called aid.

A more realistic and comprehensive classification is necessary to understand the characteristics of different kinds of aid. Here we have identified five kinds of aid, and have given them different colours. Colours are a useful way of undertaking (and remembering) a classification. In the WTO, for example, subsidies in general are identified by colour-coded boxes, for example green (permitted), amber (slow down – i.e. be reduced) and red (forbidden). There is also a green/blue box (i.e. for reduction) for agriculture subsidies that are linked to programmes to limit agricultural production.

Using rainbow colours as a pedagogical device, aid can be placed on a continuum from left to right, starting with Purple Aid (based on the principle of solidarity), Green/Blue Aid (based on the provision of global public goods), Yellow Aid (based on the principle of geopolitical strategic and security interests), Orange Aid (based on the commercial principle), and Red Aid (based on an ideological principle). Table 2 gives some examples of each of these different kinds of aid.

The pseudo-problem of coherence in donor countries

The problem in the donor countries of coherence in the use and disbursement of ODA arises primarily for two reasons:

- The donors have no proper classification of aid. By leaving out the political or military aspects of aid, the OECD-DAC definition leaves out probably the most important aspect of Western aid to developing countries.
- When conflicts about priorities arise between the various government ministries within the donor countries, it is the hierarchy of government that determines where aid should go and for what purpose. The ministry responsible for development is usually on the lowest rung.

In reality, it is a pseudo problem. The aid industry officials in the donor countries are usually located in the development ministries. They are often liberals or social-democrats and could well be the authors behind the Paris Declaration; they are constantly in argument with their counterparts in other ministries. Whatever the nature of the internal debates within governments of donor countries, it is fair to argue that considerations of *realpolitik* and the protection or promotion of national commercial interests far outweigh those of benevolence or charity. At the end of the day, when the chips are down, the coherence is primarily determined by political considerations.

1 Red Aid – ideological aid

We define Red Aid as aid that is aimed at encouraging or supporting a particular ideological viewpoint among the governments and/or peoples of the recipient countries. This is not peculiar to contemporary times. This kind of aid has been around since

Table 2 The five different kinds of aid

Aid colours	Purple	Green/Blue
Organising principle	Solidarity	Provision of global public goods
Examples	Empowering people	Compensatory funds
	Building resistance against domination	Untied grants
	Building knowledge centres	Untied humanitarian aid
	Raising awareness	Untied emergency aid
	Bringing issues to public domain	Untied technical transfer
	Providing alternative strategies	Untied aid for trade
Donors and recipient ministries	Usually head of state	Inter-ministerial

before the Romans and the ancient Greeks. More recently, but still before our own times, Red Aid during the colonial era was well articulated in Rudyard Kipling's poem 'The White Man's Burden' and was used to create norms and patterns of thought and behaviour in the receiving or target countries and institutions of governance, supplemented by educational and religious institutions – all aimed at creating and supporting the idea that the White Man knew what was best for the colonised peoples, that his ways of thought and action were superior, and that it was for the benefit of the colonised peoples to think like the White Man. This is, of course, a general characterisation of a complex process the subtleties of which are best captured in the late Edward Said's seminal book *Orientalism*.[17] In our own time, and in relation to the aid industry, the essence of this argument is well captured by William Easterly's *The White Man's Burden*.[18]

Broadly speaking, ideological or Red Aid in our times has essentially three interdependent aspects:

Yellow	Orange	Red
Liberation and survival	Commercial	Ideology
Aid to nations fighting for liberation & national project	Loans	Washington consensus conditionalities
Aid to allies fighting for survival	Tied grants	Governance conditionalities
Aid to allies to back the imperial project	Tied humanitarian aid	Human rights conditionalities
Global war on terror	Tied emergency aid	Democracy conditionalities
Control of fragile states	Tied technical transfer	Rule of law conditionalities
Control of failed states	Tied aid for trade	FDI conditionalities
Defence ministry	Trade ministry	Foreign and trade ministries

- *The ideology of development*, especially when conflated with that of globalisation and market fundamentalism, and the World Bank and IMF's so-called Washington consensus
- *The ideology of human rights*, especially when narrowed down to what are called political and civil rights, to the exclusion or relative marginalisation of economic and social rights, including the right to development
- *The ideology of good governance*, especially when it is equated with norms and principles of democracy as practised in the countries of the West, many of whom never applied these principles when they were colonial powers not long ago.

Red Aid is subtler than Yellow Aid, and its effects are more lasting. That is why winning a war by military means (as in, say, Afghanistan and Iraq) is not enough; the imperial project has to go further to win the hearts and minds of the people.

The same logic applies to, for example, World Bank or donors' aid to the developing countries. It is not enough to help design their macroeconomic, monetary and fiscal policies; it is necessary to go beyond and capture the hearts and minds of the people (or at least the decision makers) so that well after the donors have withdrawn, the colonised minds continue to think in the same way. It is for this reason that there has been a palpable shift towards Red Aid in the aid portfolio of developed countries and the World Bank in the last three decades, as Figure 1 shows.

The figure shows, among other things, that:

- The Financial and Private Sector Development conditionalities have levelled out, thus indicating the donors' perceptions that they have succeeded in getting the ideas behind these accepted and incorporated within the policy framework of the recipient countries
- The conditionalities in relation to Environment and

Figure 1 Share of conditions in core IBRD loans by themes

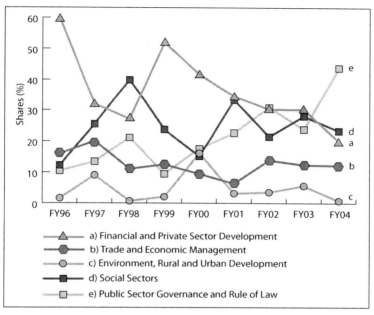

a) Financial and Private Sector Development
b) Trade and Economic Management
c) Environment, Rural and Urban Development
d) Social Sectors
e) Public Sector Governance and Rule of Law

Source of data: ALCID, World Bank (2005) *Review of World Bank Conditionality: Recent Trends and Practices*, Table 2

Rural and Urban Development have barely started. However, with climate change picking up on the global agenda, and depending on whether the World Bank and the donors exercise control over the funds for climate change, this aspect is likely to show an upward trend

• The Public Sector and Governance and Rule of Law conditionalities have steadily increased (from 10 per cent to 45 per cent) between 1996 and 2004, indicating donors' perceptions that it is bad governance in the recipient countries that is to blame for the persistence of poverty, thus justifying greater donor interference in matters of governance and aid effectiveness.

It is not accidental, therefore, that during 2003–05 the rich countries committed $1.3 billion of ODA funds to improving governance in the least developed countries (LDCs), and only $12 million to agricultural improvement.[19]

Figure 1 demonstrates the general pattern of what I call the imperial project or the imperial factor. Historically, all imperial projects begin with military conquest, then with economic restructuring so that the colonised country's economy services the needs of the imperial nations, and finally ideological conversion of the colonised leadership and population through education, training, etc. It is the same pattern with the present development aid architecture. As Figure 1 (drawn from World Bank data) shows, the economic restructuring process is more or less over. The donor countries' conditionalities on this front have reached their equilibrium. What is not in place, however, is the governance aspect of development. This rhetorically means matters such as building democratic institutions modelled on Western experience, the observance of human rights especially civil and political rights, the rule of law, and the accountability of public sector expenditure. This is what underlies the motivation and justification of much of Northern aid. However, it is also a policy of 'tied aid', no less imperial than aid that seeks to impose certain macroeconomic policies.

Knowledge transfer as the key ingredient of Red Aid

Whilst Yellow Aid takes the form of military hardware and political intervention for regime change or regime sustenance, Red Aid takes the form of 'knowledge software' and is aimed at capturing the hearts and minds of people. Once embedded in the minds of the people, it takes a long time – decades if not hundreds of years – to unshackle the 'thinking lock-in', cleanse the mind of received knowledge and turn to a new paradigm of thought and knowledge production. (This is one reason why it is so difficult to put across the essential message of this monograph: the OECD-World Bank have captured the knowledge domain of the development literature.)

This knowledge is transferred to developing countries in many forms, such as technical assistance (for example, development consultants), grants-in-aid for research and scholarship, aid to develop educational curricula and development strategies, capacity building – all these as conceptualised and articulated by the dominant discourse on development, democracy, human rights, good governance, etc.

Beyond capturing the hearts and minds of the governments and peoples so assisted, Red Aid sets out to establish norms and institutions for operationalising those norms, and sanctions against those who violate them. These institutions are created at various levels – village (for example, the replacement of indigenous 'chiefs' with local councils), sub-national, national, regional, continental and global. At the global level, for example, there are special courts and tribunals set up to try and punish those in the South that have (or are perceived to have) violated these norms (for example, on human rights). Ignored and generally left free of penalty are those in the North that are guilty of similar, or worse, crimes, either in the past or in the present.

Key difference between traditional and new donors

This is where the major difference lies between Western aid to Africa, for example, and Chinese or Indian aid. The latter refuse to be drawn into using aid to interfere in the internal governance of the recipient countries. Attempts on the part of the traditional donors to persuade China, for example, to use its aid to the Sudan or Zimbabwe to influence the political direction in these countries and their observance of human rights and the rule of law (as conceptualised by the West) have met with stern resistance from China.

Two caveats

Having said this, it is necessary to introduce two caveats about confusing universal values with imperial interests in order to give a more balanced perspective on this sensitive and complex subject.

First, it is important to distil out of the imperially imposed system of values those values that are indeed universal, and recognised in all cultures and civilisations, though in different forms and spiritual languages. There are aspects of cultural and spiritual values that acquire universal validity and recognition through multicultural interaction and mutual learning in which no culture is superior to others. The imperial project that seeks to impose nationally or regionally specific values and the thinking of the donors to serve imperial interests must be distinguished from this broader historical vision.

Second, whilst knowledge transfer takes place (or is perceived to take place) as from the North to the South, it is also necessary to acknowledge that science, innovation, and the development of productive forces are not Western inventions. It is true that since the Industrial Revolution, and in more recent times, the contributions in this area made by companies and publicly funded research institutions in these countries are truly phenomenal, but the West's Renaissance and Industrial Revolution were built on the scientific, technological, social, philosophical and cultural advances of non-Western civilisations from Africa, the Middle East and from even further afield such as the present Latin America, India and China. Even today it is impossible, for example, for the pharmaceutical or the agricultural seeds industries to make innovations in their respective fields without the biogenetic resources and knowledge systems of the South.

If these two caveats are placed against the hegemonic and one-sided transfer of knowledge and institutions from the North to the South, and if the hubris of Western civilisation ('It is a good idea' as Gandhi once said) is put into its proper historical and 'civilising' context, then there is still some hope that in our own times (going beyond the present generation) we could build a more multicultural, tolerant and humane civilisation.

2 Orange Aid – commercial aid or non-developmental development aid

Orange Aid should not be classified as aid. Consider the following as examples:

- Commercial loans and grants
- Tied humanitarian aid
- Tied emergency aid
- Tied debt relief or debt cancellations
- Tied technology transfers
- Tied aid for trade
- Export credit schemes established to assist companies based in industrialised countries to invest in and export to developing countries
- Microcredit schemes that require returns to investors.

Let us elaborate on a few of these.

On the issue of commercial loans, there is very little to argue about. These are not aid in any sense of the term. Commercial loans are often presented as win-win forms of financial transfers. In many cases, however, these are transactions undertaken by parties in 'partnership' that have a lopsided or asymmetrical relationship based on power and access to information, resources and knowledge. But even if these transactions were genuinely win-win, why should it be regarded as aid? If indeed both parties are winning, who is aiding whom? Furthermore, if these loans have to be paid back, they create a debt situation that could be worse than the loan itself. Why, then, should this kind of loan be considered as aid at all?

The DAC-OECD treats loans that have a 25 per cent grant element as development aid. But both grants and concessionary loans lose value as aid if the monies are then tied to procurement from the donor country or countries. This is a subject well covered in the aid literature. What is not covered is that there are often explicit or implicit ideological conditions tied to these concessionary loans and grants. Every bit of negotiated grant or concessionary loan may not state these conditions explicitly, but they are undertaken in the overall context of implicit 'understandings': that the recipient country needs to create an enabling environment for foreign investments, that it needs, for example, to open up its economy to trade and financial liberalisation, that it must not undertake any nationalisation or appropriation of assets tied up with the grants of loans without market-based full compensation, that intellectual property rights must be protected, that the country needs to make other inward adjustments, and so on. In other words, through conditionalities, commercial aid is turned into Red Aid. The prevalence of these tied conditions is so universal that they are taken for granted as standard practices of all normal trading and investments. Indeed, donors argue that these conditions, whether or not explicitly stated, are often accepted by the recipients. But to consider any of these as part of aid is misusing the concept of aid. If business is business why call it aid? Why call a spade a shovel?

What is true about ideologically tied loans and grants is generally true about all other forms of Orange Aid, namely, tied humanitarian aid, tied emergency aid, tied debt relief or debt cancellations, tied technology transfers, and tied aid for trade. There is no need to labour the point.

However, beside ideologically tied aid there are other kinds of Orange Aid that need to be considered. These might be considered as accounting aid, or aid to balance the books in national accounting. Two concrete examples may help to understand this accounting concept of aid – namely, debt relief treated as development aid, and expenses incurred by donor/host countries on the welfare of refugees coming from the South.

In some traditional calculations, in the case of the United Kingdom for example, debt cancellations are counted as development aid. This is what happened, for example, with the debt relief provided to many African and other LDC countries following the Gleneagles G8 meeting in 2005. Some people have argued that this cannot be described as aid. How can debt cancellation be aid, they argue, when it adds nothing to the development effort, except to pay back the debt which many of these poor countries were not in a position to pay in any case. Also, when loans with a 25 per cent grant are accounted for as aid, how can the cancellation of the grant element be counted again as aid? In sound accounting an income or expenditure should be counted only once – otherwise it is regarded as fraud.

One viewpoint is that debt relief, from a certain national and accounting perspective, is indeed aid. From the point of the UK taxpayers, for example, debt cancellation may well be aid. As far as the British taxpayer is concerned, the forgiven debt is unrequited debt, and constitutes a sacrifice. Whether the debtor countries were ever going to be able to repay that debt is irrelevant to the argument. Furthermore, it is not only in order to align accounting figures in the national budget (accountants must get their book entries completed), but also for domestic *political* consumption that the UK government, and other donors, are obliged to show their electorate that debt cancellations are constituted as aid to the poor. The donor governments do not find any merit in stating that much of this debt was historical or even intergenerational debt and was not incurred by the existing regimes or their poor.

On the other hand, of course, from the developing country perspective (shared by those in the civil society in the North campaigning on the issue of debt equity), the question of how the debt arose in the first place is an equally important political question. If it arose, for example, as a result of a corrupt third world regime borrowing heavily from a Western source (private or public) to keep itself in power, and to suppress the people (or deny them basic human rights, as for example, during apartheid in South Africa), then that debt is odious and should not, it is argued, be paid back in any case.[20]

Let us take a second case – that of expenditure undertaken in the North to help settle political or economic refugees from the South (or fees and allowances paid to foreign students in the North). Some NGOs (and not only NGOs) argue that is not development aid, because all those monies are spent, after all, in the North. The money does not go to the South. The counter argument is that these refugees (most of them economic refugees) are from the South, and their geographic relocation in the North does not alter that reality. It is the people of the South, it is argued, who benefit from these expenses incurred from the national coffers, and the host country incurs sacrifices.

The deeper question, however, is neither geographic nor a matter of accounting; it is political. The question to ask is why people in many developing countries feel compelled to leave their home and hearth and take refuge in the North. Of course, there can be any number of explanations from, for example, national ones (civil wars, oppressive governments, a collapsing economy, etc) to systemic ones (imperial wars, impoverishing effects, for example, of adverse terms of trade or of IMF-World Bank initiated structural adjustment programmes) and even pull factors (where the North may lure economic refugees from the South for low-wage, bottom-of-the-ladder jobs which their domestic population does not want to undertake). Whatever the merits of each of these arguments, the point really is that it is, in essence, a matter of political economy, not of geography nor accounting.

To conclude, it is argued here that all ideologically tied grants and part-grant bearing loans (concessional loans), and items of accounting aid are self-serving and development distorting. These are not part of development aid.

3 Yellow Aid – military and political aid

According to most literature, the United Nations and the OECD's definition, military assistance is not considered as part of development aid. The question is: Why not? We raise the issue of military and political aid afresh, and ask if it is legitimate (and under what circumstances it is legitimate) to consider military and political aid as indeed part of development aid.

The traditional argument about military or political aid is

clouded by moral and strategic considerations that make a dispassionate discussion difficult. Some of these considerations are that:

- Military or political aid is self-serving; it serves the interest of the provider of military hardware and military interventions
- It provides support to the regimes in the country or the region assisted; many of these regimes or governments use the weapons to suppress their own people or people in the region
- Alternatively, military and political aid is often aimed at supporting opposition political parties or tendencies
- Whilst military aid may generate some employment in aid recipient countries in the form of, for example, manufacturing weapons or providing services to military personnel, its essential purpose is to destroy life and property and not to create life or increase the productivity of the economy
- The millions that are spent on military aid should, instead, be spent on, for example, feeding children in poor countries, or providing them with vaccines against diseases, or, in another context, on mitigation or adaptation measures against climate change.

For these reasons (among others), it is argued that Yellow Aid cannot be classified as development aid. The moral strength of this line of reasoning is undeniable. Obviously, for example, if the money spent on military aid were used instead for food and medicines for children, or for climate change adaptation and mitigation of greenhouse gas emissions, we would live in a different – nicer – world, with probably nobody dying of hunger or preventable diseases, and with the additional gift of a sustainable climate.

However, there are at least four fallacies in the argument:

- First, the argument is tautological. Define military aid as not developmental and, on the basis of that definition, deny that it belongs to the category of aid.
- Second, the argument ignores the possibility that military aid may have its own developmental rationale (see below).
- Third, the moral argument that military aid should be converted into, for example, support for children's education can also apply to other types of aid. Why should technical aid, for example, that pays for expensive consultants to come to Africa from the developed countries to give advice on development not be turned instead into direct support to pay for medicines for the children of the poor?
- Finally, classifying Yellow Aid as 'not aid' puts it beyond the pale of proper discussion. Military or political aid should be considered and discussed like any other aid, and not pushed under the rug, and out of sight of intelligent discourse. This is morally wrong.

It might be argued that this thinking goes against all conventional wisdom, against all prevalent notions of aid that exclude military aid as being not developmental. This is indeed part of our argument, namely that it is necessary to think outside the box and liberate minds from decades of false reasoning on what should and should not be considered as aid. Military and political aid is part of day-to-day reality, and without it some countries and regimes might not even survive, let alone develop.

Take the example of US military aid to Israel, at least from the American and Israeli point of view. Without US military assistance, Israel might in all probability not even exist as a country. Development of its economy comes second, its very survival and security, surely, comes first; it is the prerequisite for its economic development. The US Congress regularly votes huge sums of money in military aid to Israel (among others). To deny that military aid is 'aid' is to deny the connection between security and development.

Whilst Israel's existence as a country is the issue here, in other similar situations, it is more a case of the survival of a regime or a system of governance. Thus, for example, if the US withdraws its military aid to Afghanistan or Iraq, the present regimes of governance could collapse, even if the countries would no doubt continue to exist.

Let us take one step further. What applies to Afghanistan or Iraq at the country level also applies at a regional or even continental level. For example, one could argue that America's planned African Command (AFRICOM), with an increased US military presence on the continent, may be for the protection of a particular type of African regime of governance and provision of security from terrorist threat. One might counter argue, on moral or political grounds, that African countries should not accept this kind of aid from the US. But for those African governments which do share with the US a common perception of the terrorist threat, and therefore accept the terms of this partnership, this kind of assistance may well qualify as aid.

Having gone this far in the argument, then, let us nonetheless ask the question: Is all Yellow Aid developmental? Because the peace and security of a country and a region are, indisputably, the fundamental basis for development, does it then mean that all Yellow Aid is developmental?

That, however, is not the case. Not all Yellow Aid is developmental, and whether it is or it is not depends on where one stands, *politically*, on the substantial issue at stake. *Whether military and political aid may legitimately be described as developmental depends on just one factor, and one factor only. It depends on whether that form of aid serves to free the ordinary people of a nation or a region from external or foreign bondage.* Some elaboration of this is obviously necessary.

Looking back into history, I would argue that the military aid provided by, for example, the NATO countries to Angola and

South Africa during their peoples' struggles for liberation from colonial and apartheid rule was not developmental aid to the people of these countries. On the other hand, assistance provided by Cuba, China and the then Soviet Union to the people of Angola and South Africa qualifies as developmental aid.

I am aware that simple as it may sound, this statement is a minefield of contentious issues that cross the borders of history, geography, politics, ideology, economics and ethics. And that is the whole point of this study – *namely, that to abstract aid from the context of geography, history, politics and ethics is itself wrong.* In other words, as the example above shows, military or political aid (or for that matter any kind of aid) is not a statistical abstraction. It is a political matter, and it involves political values and judgments. However, it is not a matter of purely subjective or individual personal choice. Neither NATO's decision to help sustain Portuguese rule in Angola or the apartheid regime in South Africa, nor Cuba's decision to help the forces of liberation in these countries, was a matter of personal choice between individuals making decisions in their respective governments. It was, on both sides, a political decision made at a national level.

Those who are outside the perimeters of government decision making (media agents, academics, historians, non-governmental organisations, etc) may think differently from their own governments. They, too, have to make a decision on how they view the situation from their political-ethical standpoint. Many in the US and Europe may well agree with my judgment that NATO's intervention in Angola prior to the country's liberation in 1975 was counter-developmental, and that US intervention in Vietnam was also counter-developmental. Or, to give an example from a different historical context and depending on one's political perspective, one might regard the millions spent by George Soros in order to 'liberate' countries of Central and Eastern Europe from the 'tyranny' of Communist regimes as development aid.

So this seems like a good moment to say that the question of defining aid as developmental is not a neutral or value free exercise. It is, essentially, a political exercise. And, as all political exercises go, there are at least two sides to every issue. What kind of Yellow Aid qualifies to be called developmental depends not on what the donor might say or do, but on its effects, in this case, on freeing the human potential and resource of a nation for self-development. If the self-development, self-determination, of nations is compromised by aid, then that kind of aid is counter-developmental. It is for this reason that the issue of ownership has loomed so large in recent literature on aid, an issue to which we come later when we discuss the Paris Declaration on Aid Effectiveness.

When the UN, the DAC-OECD or the NGOs decide to leave (the sizeable) military aid out of their equation, they are simply ducking the issue. Indeed, it gets powerful countries off the hook. The huge amount of NATO aid and the relatively small amount of Cuban aid given at great sacrifice are put in the same basket and thrown out to sea as not being development aid. Leaving military or political aid out of the traditional definition of development aid is itself a political act designed to narrow the scope of aid and hence allow for the evasion of questions regarding the direction, quantity and impact of military aid as compared to other types of aid. It also leaves one free to take the moralistic position that 'all military aid is bad' and should be diverted to more useful purposes.

So, to conclude this section, here is the start of defining development aid in its proper historical and political context, from the perspective of the South. The South, it might be added here, is a broader category than a geographic understanding might suggest. There are individuals and groups of individuals in the North who take political positions on a whole range of matters – from liberation from colonial and apartheid rule, to economic development, to climate change – that are similar (in some cases identical) to similarly inclined individuals and groups of individuals in the South.

If the argument so far is followed, without the dogmatic

shackles of traditional depoliticised and abstract thinking based on OECD's definition of aid, then the argument with respect to other colours of aid will be easier to understand.

4 Green/Blue Aid – provision of global public goods

Green/Blue Aid, or the provision of global public goods (GPGs), is defined broadly to mean all forms of financial or technical and technological transfers that are for genuinely humanitarian purposes; or arising out of legal obligations undertaken in internationally agreed commitments for the sake of the common good; or for what we describe as 'compensatory finance', to redress existing or historical inequities in the system.

The three forms of Green/Blue Aid on a continuum are illustrated in Figure 2.

Figure 2 The three forms of Green/Blue Aid

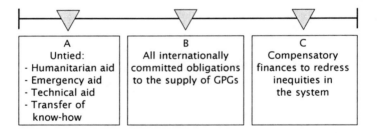

A Untied: - Humanitarian aid - Emergency aid - Technical aid - Transfer of know-how	B All internationally committed obligations to the supply of GPGs	C Compensatory finances to redress inequities in the system

Given the earlier discussion on tied loans, grants, debt relief, and expenditure on the welfare of refugees, lengthy argument is not necessary to explain why, when all these come as untied aid – that is, they are not tied to any procurement or ideological conditions – and when their content and use are fully determined by the recipient countries, it is justifiable to classify these as aid for genuine humanitarian reasons or to fulfil internationally agreed commitments for global public goods.

The concept of global public goods was first introduced in the context of debates within the World Bank and the United Nations Development Programme (UNDP) towards the early part of the 2000s.[21] Jetin and Denys give a detailed taxonomy of GPGs.[22] The following examples demonstrate its rich, wide-ranging taxonomy:

- Extinguishing forest fires and flood control, as intra-generational regional pure public goods
- Depolluting rivers and allocation of electromagnetic wave bands, as intragenerational regional impure public goods
- Cleaning up toxic waste, protecting the ozone layer and control and eradication of epidemics, as intergenerational global pure public goods
- Reduction in volatile organic compounds and ensuring global financial stability as intergenerational global impure public goods.

The rationale behind the taxonomy is complex, but the argument behind describing these as GPGs is reasonable – namely, goods in the public domain have a fairly universal impact and are there for all to consume. Therefore, providing for them cannot be the responsibility of a single nation but a collectivity of them, whether at regional or global level. Neither are they all the responsibility of a single generation; they go beyond the present generation.

The implication of this argument is obvious. It is that when countries provide financial or technological resources for GPGs, they are not doing any favours to another nation. Provisioning of GPGs is often driven by self-interest. Countries chose to finance GPGs because they stand to benefit from them nationally. For instance, protection of the ozone layer has clear national benefits. They are doing favours to themselves. In other cases, these countries are simply fulfilling certain obligations they have towards the international community measured, for example, in terms of historical responsibility, present responsibility and capacity to make contributions to the GPGs on the principle of 'common but differentiated responsibility' agreed by the negotiating parties at the 1992 Rio Environment and Development Conference. In other words, the GPGs are not part of the aid package. If the developed countries provide assistance to the developing countries (for example, through the Global Environment Fund or through the Clean Development Mechanism) to encourage them to adopt low emissions technologies, such assistance should not be treated as part of aid.

Compensatory finance

What is compensatory finance? It is compensatory finance when the obligation to transfer funds is linked to a historical responsibility, or obligation arising out of an inequity as a result of history or current trading. A quick example that comes to mind is the compensatory finance that, for example, the people of Germany have provided the Jewish people, arising out of the injustice done to them during the anti-Semitic Hitler regime.

The principle is also well recognised, for example, in the UN Framework Convention on Climate Change (UNFCCC), where developed countries have both a historical responsibility to compensate the developing countries for the damage they (the developed countries) have caused to the environment during their period of industrialisation. This historical responsibility is reflected in the UNFCCC's treaty provisions that oblige developed countries to provide new and additional financial flows (as well as technology transfers) to developing countries to support the latter's costs for implementing the UNFCCC and to undertake climate adaptation. To date, however, developed countries have not complied with such historical responsibility and treaty obligation to provide climate change-related compensatory finance.

Besides examples related to climate change, there are other claims that might legitimately be classified as compensatory finance. One of these relates to the current negotiations between the African, Caribbean and Pacific (ACP) countries and the European Union for Economic Partnership Agreements (EPAs).

Though the negotiations are conducted in the technical jargon of trade officials, there is a larger political dimension that the political leaders of ACP countries and the EU cannot sweep under the carpet. Let us recall certain aspects of this historical legacy:

- A built-in structural division of labour based on the ACP countries providing human beings in the form of commodities, super-exploited wage labour, and grossly under-priced natural resources. These were needed for the industrialisation of Europe from the 17th to the 20th centuries
- Imbalanced trade and a balance of payments deficit resulting from Europe's comparative advantage in manufactured products, equipment, services (such as shipping, insurance and banking) and products secured under intellectual property rights, arising out of this historical division of labour
- The ensuing liberation struggle (from the end of the First World War to the liberation of South Africa in 1994) at enormous cost, particularly to people in Africa, from which they have not yet fully recovered
- The Cotonou and previous agreements that cemented in place a colonial-type, structured asymmetrical relationship over production and trade.

One outcome of the EU and ACP countries joining the WTO is that they now face the prospect of eliminating the trading 'preferences' that have developed under this legacy in order to be compatible with the trading norms of the WTO. According to a United Nations Economic Commission for Africa (UNECA) study, African countries would stand to lose $1.9 billion in tariff revenue.[23] Furthermore, research by the Commonwealth Secretariat estimates that the overall costs for a minimum level of restructuring adjustment support required by ACP countries is €9.2 billion over ten years.[24] This does not take into account job losses and the effects of a negative balance of payments.

The question is: Who bears the cost of these forced adjustments on the ACP countries? We are of the view that the EU has the responsibility to compensate the ACP countries for any losses they suffer as a result of a forcible adjustment to a new trade regime from a historically created dependent relationship that Europe had created with its former colonies. These deeply embedded, imbalanced structured relationships created over 300 years of history cannot simply be broken in 50 or 60 years and, in any case, not until the erstwhile colonies have put in place a proper exit strategy from aid dependence – the subject of this monograph.

5 Purple Aid – principle of solidarity

Purple Aid is that which is provided for reasons of solidarity with the people(s) of the receiving countries. This can be placed along an escalator continuum:

6 Providing alternative strategies

5 Helping resistance against domination

4 Empowering people

3 Building knowledge centres

2 Bringing issues to public domain

1 Raising awareness

The escalator continuum shows the degree and intensity of solidarity, starting at the bottom step – raising awareness about an existing social or political injustice – escalating upwards until the provision of an alternative development model becomes the last step of the escalator. The first three steps of this escalator are knowledge based and the last three action based. It is not necessary to elaborate on all of these. They are well known categories. They are well understood at least by those who provide and those who receive assistance on the basis of solidarity.

The earlier discussion of Yellow Aid (military or political aid) identified the assistance provided by, for example, the Soviet

Union, China, India and Cuba to the peoples of Africa to help them liberate themselves from colonialism and apartheid, as an example of purple, or solidarity, aid. The same could also be said of the assistance that many governments in the West (especially the Nordic and Scandinavian governments) and peoples' solidarity movements – even within imperial countries – gave to fight against colonialism, apartheid, the imperial war in Vietnam, etc.

In more recent times, Purple Aid includes, for example, the help that the present government of Venezuela provides to the countries in its region in order to liberate themselves from the domination of the US or Bretton Woods institutions. Venezuela's motives can be debated, but as we argued earlier these are, in essence, political positions, depending on one's political perspectives.

Among those who provide such solidarity help are hundreds of civil society organisations in the North, who recognise a historical and moral responsibility towards peoples of a large part of this world who are poor and deprived through no fault of theirs or of their parents and previous generations. They recognise that history has been cruel to the poor, and that developed countries have a responsibility towards the poor in developing countries to help alleviate poverty. This kind of help, thus, is on the border between Purple Aid and Green/Blue Aid.

A litany of false questions and solutions

Once the preceding aid taxonomy and the political and economic logic behind it are understood, it is easy to see why the present aid industry has sponsored so many false (or pseudo-) questions and concerns around aid and aid management, and equally false (or pseudo-) solutions.

Here are a few examples of false questions which can be multiplied in manifold ways:

- Can more aid be absorbed? How can we build Africa's capacity to 'absorb' more aid? (It is obvious that this is a donor initiated, top–down and, some might

say, patronising question, and leads to building a justification for Red Aid.)

- Can rich countries afford more aid? Should rich countries give more aid? Our countries have given too much aid already to the corrupt regimes of the South. (This is a common refrain among the population of the developed countries of the North, and has no empirical foundation.)
- What can be done to help the governance of receiving countries so that they are fit to receive more aid? (This often goes under the name of 'capacity building' and is a top–down, patronising viewpoint.)

And here are some false solutions:

- Aid and trade sanctions should be used to discipline Gadaffi, Castro, Ahmadinejad, Chavez, Mugabe... (Who else?)
- Microfinancing is good for the people. (However, in practice, it is often dressed up as market ideology which, in turn, is dressed up as developmental.)
- More aid or better quality aid (e.g. budget support) is needed. (However, this is often packaged within the framework of market fundamentalism and good governance as defined by the donors.)
- What is needed is more effective administration of aid. (However, this is also usually done within the framework of market fundamentalism and good governance, as defined by the donors.)
- There should be harmonisation and aid coherence of budget with donors. (However, this can lead to the donors ganging up against aid recipients.)

And so on.

It could be an interesting exercise to ask first year undergraduate economics and social science students to scan through the vast literature on the aid industry, and make a list of the false or pseudo questions arising out of some self-serving paradigms. They should examine the incorrect hypotheses and flawed premises. They should critically look at the data collected on the basis of one-sided definitions and questionable methodologies. Finally, they should examine for whose benefit the 'solutions' are proposed.

Conclusion

In concluding this section, let me say that the importance of this part is because it challenges the current dogma about development aid. Based on a one-sided and self-serving OECD definition of ODA, the aid industry is inundated with a litany of pseudo questions, and logically, a litany of solutions that, not surprisingly, have promoted not development but perpetual aid dependence. Promoting extensive dialogues and discussions among donors and recipients in the name of aid effectiveness on this litany of false questions and solutions has only ended up perpetuating the orthodox and palpably false thinking of OECD-DAC on aid.

It is argued further here that the OECD's definition is not only seriously flawed, both in logic and when placed on the hard ground of reality, but that it is also politically inspired. Aid recipient countries are under no obligation to accept OECD's aid taxonomy, or its definition of what constitutes development. Instead, this book offers an alternative definition of development, and a radically different aid taxonomy that has roots in the history and the geopolitical reality of developing countries. Our taxonomy grows from the perspective of the politics of liberation, the politics of proactive emancipation of the potential forces of enlightenment and self-empowering knowledge that resides in every human being and within every nation's destiny.

Notes

1 OECD (2007a) 'Is it ODA?' Factsheet, May, http://www.oecd.org/dataoecd/21/21/34086975.pdf, accessed 16 July 2008.

2 This information can be downloaded from http://www.oecd.org/dac/stats/dac/directives, accessed 16 July 2008.

3 OECD (2007a) p. 1.

4 Ibid, p. 3.

5 Ibid, p. 2.

6 OECD (2007b) The Statistical Reporting Directives, http://www.oecd.org/dac/stats/dac/directives, accessed 16 July 2008.

7 Ibid.

8 Ibid.

9 UN Economic and Social Council (2008) *Trends and Progress in International Development Cooperation*, Report of the Secretary General, E/2008/59, p. 15.

10 See appendix to the Gleneagles communiqué, accessed at http://www.g8.gov.uk/servlet/Front?pagename=OpenMarket/Xcelerate/ShowPage&c=Page&cid=1078995902703.

11 Commission for Africa (2005) *Our Common Interest: Report of the Commission for Africa*, United Nations Economic Commission for Africa, http://www.uneca.org/commreport.pdf, accessed 16 July 2008.

12 Ibid, p. 90.

13 Smillie, I. (2000) 'NGOs: crisis and opportunity in the new world order', in Freedman, J. (ed) (2000) *Transforming Development: Foreign Aid for a Changing World*, Toronto, University of Toronto Press, p. 125.

14 *Financial Times* (2008) Editorial, 13 May.

15 World Bank (2008) *The Growth Report: Strategies for Sustained Growth and Inclusive Development*, http://www.growthcommission.org/storage/cgdev/documents/Report/GrowthReportfull.pdf

16 Ibid, p. 21.

17 Said, Edward (1978) *Orientalism: Western Conceptions of the Orient*, Routledge.

18 Easterly, William (2008) *The White Man's Burden: Why the West's Efforts to Aid the Rest Have Done So Much Ill and So Little Good*, New York, Penguin.

19 See UNCTAD (2007) *The Least Developing Countries Report: Knowledge, Technological Learning and Innovation for Development*, Geneva, United Nations.

20 In international law, odious debt is a legal theory which holds that debt incurred by a regime for purposes that do not serve the interest of the nation should not be enforceable. Such debts are thus considered by this doctrine to be personal debts of the regime that incurred them and not debts of the state. In some respects, the concept is analogous to the invalidity of contracts

signed under coercion. See also Adams, Patricia (1991) *Odious Debts: Loose Lending, Corruption, and the Third World's Environmental Legacy*, London, Earthscan.

21 Kaul, Inge et al (2003) *Providing Global Public Goods: Managing Globalisation*, New York, Oxford University Press.

22 Jetin, B. and Denys, L. (2005) 'Technical and legal aspects of a currency transaction tax, and its implementation in the EU', World Economy, Ecology and Development website.

23 UNECA (2006) *The Economic and Welfare Impacts of the EU-Africa Economic Partnership Agreements*, African Trade Policy Centre.

24 Dodd, Liz (2008), 'Real and hidden cost of Economic Partnership Agreements', *South Bulletin*, no. 17, p. 12.

CHAPTER 2

CASE HISTORIES
The consequences of aid dependence

Red Aid – the poisoned chalice

The effect of receiving Purple Aid (aid on a solidarity basis) or Green/Blue Aid (on the basis of genuine humanitarian aid, commitments made in respect of global public goods and compensatory finance) is empowering. These kinds of assistance help to develop self-confidence, local knowledge production and the creation of local institutions that are not tied to the imperial projects. They also help people and countries to build the courage to challenge existing power structures and knowledge monopoly in order to be liberated from their dominance. On the other hand, certain kinds of Yellow Aid (military and political assistance aimed at helping a country liberate itself from foreign domination) can be self-empowering; but there are also forms of Yellow Aid whose effect can be the enslavement of a people to the domination of a foreign power.

The most damaging types of aid, however, are Red Aid – aid tied to ideological, human rights or governance conditionalities – and Green/Blue Aid, which are premised on similar conditionalities. Dependence on these kinds of aid is disempowering. They undermine the self-confidence of the recipient countries' governments and peoples, and erode policy space. The principal reason is that these kinds of aid are tied to certain conditionalities and macroeconomic solutions, such as those that have been imposed on the recipient countries by the donors and the Bretton Woods institutions and the Paris Declaration on Aid Effectiveness.

A few examples might help to illustrate the point. I describe below two personal experiences from Southern Africa, where I worked for 23 years in the critical period from the struggles for independence through the first couple of decades after independence.

Structural adjustment: Zambia 1978–2002

Zambia got into economic difficulties during the 1970s – largely on account of externally related factors, such as falling cooper prices and the deteriorating terms of trade. The government concluded a two-year 'stabilisation programme' with the IMF in 1978. Instead of stabilising the economy, the situation worsened, inflation accelerated even faster and this severely hit all fixed-income earners, especially wage workers. In 1981 and again in 1983 Zambia concluded extended fund facility agreements with the IMF. However, because Zambia could not conform to the rigours of the IMF's eligibility criteria, only 375 million units of special drawing rights (SDR) were disbursed out of over SDR 1 billion that was negotiated. In 1986, in an attempt to meet with the IMF's conditionalities, government reduced the maize meal subsidy and this led to food riots in the Copper Belt and the death of 15 people by police action. On 1 May 1987 government suspended the structural adjustment programme (SAP).

For two years – from May 1987 to July 1989 – Zambia decided to operate its own 'growth from our resource' strategy. The New Economic Recovery Programme (NERP), as it was called, introduced major policy changes, including diversification, inflation control, rationing of foreign exchange, and reduction in import dependence. The economy improved remarkably. Agriculture grew at 21 per cent and manufacturing at 15 per cent, and the overall GDP growth rate was 6.7 per cent against the planned target of 2.2 per cent.

But then the creditors came knocking at the door. The IMF and the World Bank demanded payment of the accumulated debt of SDR 5.7 billion, plus SDR 1.2 billion in arrears and interests. Eighty-three per cent of total export of goods and services went simply to service these debts. In other words, for every dollar's worth of all the copper and other commodities Zambia exported, only 17 cents came back to the people of Zambia and 83 cents went to foreign creditors. At the same time, all other donors – including those who claimed to be friends of Zambia – cut off aid to Zambia. They said they would bring in their capital only if Zambia returned to the IMF and World Bank. Zambia was on its knees. In July 1989 Zambia abandoned NERP and came back to the IMF and World Bank's SAP. In June 1990, the government, in order to meet IMF's conditionality, again reduced the maize meal subsidy. For two weeks, there were food riots (the author was personally witness to these riots in Lusaka), which spread to Kafue and Kabwe. Twenty-six civilians and a policeman died. On 30 June 1990, there was an attempted military coup. There was little the government could do to help the people. In the 1993 elections, people voted Kaunda's government out of power, and put in the saddle a trade unionist, Frederick Chiluba, hoping he would give people what Kaunda could not. But Chiluba's hands were as much tied as Kaunda's. The World Bank, the IMF and the creditors regained control over Zambia's economy.

Under the new government, payments of arrears to the IMF were cleared as long as Zambia successfully implemented the SAP conditionalities on an annual basis. For this to happen, governments had to 'liberalise' trade, investment and dividend remittances. It had to cut down on health and education. It had to devalue the kwacha in order to encourage exports, and to attract foreign capital. It had to sell off state controlled enterprises (the collective assets of its people) to the private sector, but since only the foreign private sector had the capital to buy these, they fell into the hands of large foreign corporations; Zambia was now under the control of foreign corporations more than ever before. And part of the agreement was tax relief for the foreign companies extracting and exporting raw resources out of the country.

Nonetheless, the selling off of these assets brought relief to the economy by injecting more money into it, but it was a temporary relief for the hard pressed treasury. Soon, prices started soaring again; shortages of commodities were back; unemployment increased. The informal sector of the economy now provides for some 75 per cent to 80 per cent of the population.

In 2002 Chiluba lost when Zambians elected the late President Levy Mwanawasa as his successor.

Structural adjustment: Zimbabwe 1980–97

Zimbabwe has been so much in the news, particularly in the Western media, in recent times, and it has received such adverse publicity that the first impulse is to avoid the subject, but that would be a mistake. A country that has become a pariah state needs to be talked about so that its situation is understood objectively and dispassionately. But the main reason I bring it into this discussion is that Zimbabwe provides a very appropriate case study for the subject of this monograph. There are few such good illustrations of the best aspects of Purple and Yellow Aid (the solidarity movement in Europe, for example, during the struggle for liberation), and of the worst aspects of Red Aid.

During the unilateral declaration of independence (UDI) years (1965–80) the state of Rhodesia had instituted a policy of industrialisation for import substitution. It had managed to secure capital, technology and oil by building a network of links with sanctions breakers. Local production had increased to service the domestic market with almost 600 separate consumer items, as well as some of the military equipment to fight against the guerrillas. The guerrillas, in turn, were helped by neighbouring African countries, the Organisation of African Unity (as it then was), China, the Soviet Union, India, Cuba and a host of solidarity-based civil society organisations in Europe and America.

At independence, the new government inherited a reasonable economy, but huge social and political problems. The democratisation of the system of governance took essentially the

47

Westminster model, together with a few Marxist-Leninist structures, particularly in the relationship between the state and the ruling party. During the first decade, the state took direct action to rectify the historical imbalances against the people.

In the area of the economy, the government tried to balance the demands of maintaining production and productivity on the land, in industry and in the mines on the one hand, and on the other hand raising the standard of living of ordinary workers and communal farmers and bringing them into the mainstream of democratic politics. The government not only legitimated the formation of trade unions, but also set certain core labour standards. It abolished the colonial Master and Servants Act and set minimum wages, thus doing away with the totally arbitrary wage-setting system of the pre-independence period. Furthermore, workers could not be sacked without the permission of the Ministry of Labour and Social Services. Workers' committees were set up in work places as primary instruments of collective bargaining, and where workers were too weak or fragmented the government instituted a system of employment councils where it constituted itself as the third party between the workers and the employers in order to negotiate a fair return for workers' labour. For the first time, the workers in Zimbabwe enjoyed decent work after almost a hundred years of 'real slavery'.

On the social welfare front, the achievements were formidable.[1] For example, by 1990, major trends in public health indicated that:

- Infant mortality was reduced from 79 to 66 per 1,000, with rural and urban differentials, also reduced
- General under-five-year-old under-nutrition (weight for age) improved from 21 per cent to 12 per cent
- Maternal mortality fell from an estimated 145 per 100,000 in 1980 to 68.7 per 100,000 in 1990
- Childhood infections due to immunisable diseases were significantly reduced, while viral infection, specifically HIV, increased, and other conditions, such

as respiratory infections and diarrhoea, persisted at a relatively constant level throughout the decade

- Immunisation cover of children expanded from 25 per cent fully immunised in 1980 to 78 per cent by 1991
- Tuberculosis declined markedly in the 1980s, falling to 1 per cent of total inpatient admissions for under-one-year-olds and reaching a relatively stable 5,000–6,000 cases per year by 1989
- Sexually transmitted infections plateaued at about 850,000 new episodes per year.

On the education front:

- During the first five years of indpendence (1980–85) the enrolment expansion rates were 6.16 per cent at primary school level and 6.61 per cent at secondary school level.
- The number of primary schools increased from 2,401 in 1979 to 4,234 by 1985 and 4,723 in 1999. The number of teachers increased from 28,455 in 1980 to 63,718 by 1996, 66,502 by 1998.
- At secondary school level, expansion rates were even higher. Enrolment increased from 66,215 in 1979 to 148,690 by 1981, rising to 786,154 by 1995, and further increased to 834,880 in 1999.
- The number of secondary schools increased from 177 in 1979 to 694 in 1981 (an increase of 292.1 per cent in three years). Most of the expansion occurred in rural areas. In the 1980s up to 83–85 per cent of primary school graduates went into the first year of secondary school.

However, state paternalism created domestic deficit financing. Import liberalisation created a balance of payments problem. The government introduced foreign exchange rationing as a means of dealing with the situation. Advised (ill-advised, as it later turned out) by experts, the government sought assistance from the IMF. The first stand-by agreement with the IMF in 1983 led to the devaluation of the Zimbabwean dollar and other measures of austerity. This was the first step on the slippery road to dependence on external forces to solve national problems. Very few in the government or the ZANU-PF party really understood what the IMF represented. It was seen as a neutral agent that would help solve the temporary balance of payments problem. The IMF's seal of approval was also seen as necessary to attract foreign capital. Thus, within five years of independence, the state made a conscious political decision to shift from relying on the people to relying on donor funds.

Once the state decided to externalise its solutions, an export-oriented strategy was the next step. The alternative would have been to develop a strong domestic and regional market based on the local needs of the people, giving more and more power to the people to run farms, factories and mines. This route was not taken. Instead, the government reversed the essentially internally oriented state of the UDI period so that it became an externally oriented one. The adoption of an orthodox economic structural adjustment programme (known by the acronym ESAP) in 1991 entailed a fundamental shift from the state intervention system to one largely driven by market forces. A detailed statement,[2] was published in early 1991 as an input into a meeting of donors held in Paris in February that year. It was only after the Paris meeting that there were pledges of financial support from donors. The political dynamism for development henceforth shifted from Harare to Paris, from the people to the donors. The assumption was that ESAP would raise investment levels, thereby facilitating higher growth rates, employment creation and uplifting the standard of living of the majority of the people.

The key targets of ESAP were to:

- Achieve GDP growth of 5 per cent during 1991–95
- Raise savings to 25 per cent of GDP
- Raise investment to 25 per cent of GDP
- Achieve export growth of 9 per cent per annum
- Reduce the budget deficit from over 10 per cent of GDP to 5 per cent by 1995

- Reduce inflation from 17.7 per cent to 10 per cent by 1995.

To achieve these, the main components of the economic reform programme were competition enhancing measures, including trade and exchange rate liberalisation, domestic deregulation and financial sector and institutional reforms pertaining to fiscal reform. The fiscal reforms encompassed fiscal and parastatals' deficit reduction and the privatisation and commercialisation of public enterprises. It also included, significantly, measures to mitigate the social costs of adjustment through the Social Dimension of Adjustment Programme. It established a Social Development Fund (SDF) which provided for financial assistance to households earning less than Z$400 per month to help them meet the increased user costs for education and health associated with ESAP. It also provided a small income supplement to offset the effects of deregulation of basic food prices. What is significant about the social fund concept is its implied recognition that the cost of adjustment would have to be borne by the poorer classes. The possibility of social unrest was already being recognised.

There was thus a *shift from state paternalism to donor paternalism*. From then on, social security was a function not of the state budget but of external funding. The allocation to the SDF from the central government budget rose from its initial Z$20 million in 1992/93 to Z$150 million the following year, but fell to Z$50 million by 1995/96.

The donor funding which had been anticipated in support of this programme fell short of expectations. The World Bank and the IMF were erratic in their disbursement of promised loans to Zimbabwe, making these conditional on political performance, such as on the land issue or defence spending, and on the fulfilment of certain fiscal, monetary and other conditions as part of the ESAP agreements. The low inflows of grants of Z$1.5 billion against a target of Z$2.7 billion, as a result of the lower than expected disbursement of funds by donors, as well as a negative net foreign financing of Z$3.4 billion, against a target of

Z$3.5 billion, resulted in extensive borrowing from the domestic market. A total of Z$13.2 billion was borrowed on the domestic market, against a target of Z$9.2 billion.

The combined effect of high budget deficits, a depreciating exchange rate, the decontrolling of prices, the removal of subsidies and a poor supply response delivered high levels of inflation. Inflation rose from 15.5 per cent in 1990, peaking at 42.1 per cent in 1992, before falling to 18.8 per cent by 1997. Following high imports, the refusal of the IMF to disburse funds, and currency speculation, the Zimbabwe dollar suffered a massive depreciation of over 40 per cent to the US dollar on 'black Friday' – 14 November 1997. By October 1999, inflation had risen to an all time high of 70.4 per cent. This necessitated the maintenance of excessively high interest rates, above 60 per cent, thus making it practically impossible for industry to borrow money for sustaining itself, let alone for development.

Ironically, instead of increasing exports, it was imports that rose. Exports grew at an annual average rate of only 2.1 per cent during the period 1991–98, against a targeted rate of 9 per cent per annum. Imports rose at an annual average rate of 4.9 per cent during the same period. For example, in September 1999 exports amounted to US$28.5 million, against imports of US$55 million. Manufacturing had been the most protected sector before the trade reforms, so liberalisation had the most negative effects here in the form of de-industrialisation. In 1997/98, manufacturing's share of GDP had fallen to less than 16 per cent for the first time since 1960, compared to an average of 25 per cent in the 1970s–80s. The sector had completely stagnated since the introduction of ESAP and the relaxation of import controls. The high interest rates and the cost of foreign currency penalised the manufacturing sector to an extent that even good rains, which usually stimulated manufacturing growth, did not manage to stir its recovery. The textiles, clothing, footwear, wood and furniture, paper, printing and publishing, and transport and equipment industries were all badly hit.

The effect of financial liberalisation

Through Zimbabwe's acceptance of Article VIII of the IMF's Article of Agreement on 2 January 1995 the government committed itself to maintaining a liberalised current account. Exchange control regulations were substantially modified to allow for large increases in business and holiday travel allowances. The establishment of foreign exchange bureaux was allowed and the private sector was permitted to borrow up to US$5 million from abroad without having to seek the approval of the External Loans Coordinating Committee. Restrictions on the remittance of new dividends by foreign companies were abolished in January 1995 with past dividends unblocked over a period of three years. To facilitate sufficiently early implementation of investment projects, domestic borrowing limits for foreign investors were removed. With effect from June 1993, foreign investors were allowed to buy up to 25 per cent (later increased to 40 per cent) of the equity of any company listed on the Zimbabwe Stock Exchange. Foreign investors were also permitted to participate at the primary issue of the stocks, and dividends from these investments qualify for 100 per cent remittance. Restrictions on the use of surplus funds and the interest cap on them were removed, freeing such funds for investment in the market at the ruling market price.[3]

In all, the opening of the financial and banking sector and partial liberalisation of the capital market created greater uncertainty in the financial sector and increased the attractiveness of purely speculative as against productive investment. Financial liberalisation brought in new, mostly portfolio capital, not greenfield investments. On the contrary, the financial sector sucked up most of the local savings as well as off-shore speculative funds, increasing their time deposits from a trivial $3.8 billion in 1985 to a staggering $47.2 billion in 1997. Liberalisation increased competition and new instruments for financing enterprises, but it also sent to the wall some indigenous banks that could not face the competition from foreign banks. Financial liberalisation also did not help small and medium scale enterprises. On the contrary, development finance was marginalised, and with the restructuring of the Agricultural Finance Corporation the communal farming sector no longer had a viable credit institution that could advance seasonal and development credit to them. Financial liberalisation spawned the rise of a small but significant local financial oligarchy, one of the few groups that benefited from ESAP. In sum, the overall effect of financial and partial capital liberalisation was negative, as the share of wages in gross domestic income declined from 54 per cent in 1987 to 39 per cent by 1997, while the share of profits rose from 47 per cent in 1987 to 63 per cent by 1996.[4]

What broke the camel's back (literally) was the land issue. In 1996 a land commission set up by the government had made recommendations on how to move forward on this very sensitive and urgent issue. The government, however, was slow to take action. Early in 1997, some farm workers decided to take direct mass action. They burned some farms and threatened some white farmers with violence. The ex-combatants, driven to poverty largely because of ESAP, organised themselves into a lobby, called the War Veterans. They claimed some 40,000 members. Between March and October they organised a series of street demonstrations all across the country, demanding an audience with the party chairman and the country's president. The president avoided them for months not knowing what to do with them, but when the street situation began to get out of hand, he finally relented. In October, he agreed to pay an immediate gratuity of Z$50,000 to each legitimate ex-combatant, plus $2,000 per month for life, plus a share in the land when the time came for its allocation, and educational and health benefits for their children.

This started a chain reaction. First was the World Bank, which immediately announced that it was temporarily withholding the disbursement of $700 million until the government gave assurances that this huge payment to the ex-combatants would not affect the government deficit. The other donors followed suit hard on the heels of the IMF and World Bank. The European Commission announced that it was withholding the second tranche of $600 million that had been agreed in 1994 until the government gave assurances that the ex-combatant payments of nearly Z$2 billion were found by fiscal means and not by borrowing from the market. Of concern to the donor community was the fact that the government debt of nearly Z$60 billion already constituted some 68 per cent of GDP.

Pressed by the donors on the one hand and on the other by the ex-combatants' demand for immediate cash payments before Christmas, the government resorted to fiscal means to raise money for the ex-combatants. It brought an emergency bill to parliament to introduce a 5 per cent levy on all income, a 2.5 per cent increase in sales tax, a 5 per cent increase on electricity, and 20 cents per litre increase on fuel. In December 1997, however, at the ZANU-PF Party Congress the delegates, mostly rural, rejected the increased levies. They also demanded immediate land reform. The party leadership, now in panic, announced that the government would take 5 million hectares of land from about 1,500 designated farms to settle the landless.

There was immediate reaction from the donors. A visiting British minister told the press that Britain did not look favourably at this land takeover by the government, and that the present generation of Britons had no responsibility for what their ancestors had done in Rhodesia, nor did the British government feel obliged to give money for the land takeover, as promised earlier. At the same time, the peasants were pressing for land reform, the ex-combatants were pressing for immediate payment of their compensation, and the workers, smarting under the effects of ESAP, were waiting for wage negotiations to begin to adjust their falling effective wages, and were angry that they were being asked to shoulder the burden of the war veterans' compensation. There emerged a crisis within the state itself. In January 1998, civil servants threatened to repeat their 1996 unprecedented strike if government did not honour the agreed pay increase by 35 per cent. The government was thus caught on all sides.

In November 1997 rumours – fuelled over the internet originating from South Africa – spread that the visiting IMF team had left Zimbabwe on account of their frustration with the government. Coming as it did in the wake of the currency crisis in East Asia, the rumour aggravated the already nervous economic climate. Already, there was a serious balance of payments deficit arising out of falling exports and increasing imports over the six months to November. Speculators, as is their wont, took their money out, and new money that was supposed to come in from outside (for example, for crop finance) was held back. The Zimbabwe currency came under siege, and on 14 November, it crashed by nearly 40 per cent to the US dollar.

Within days the grain millers announced a 25 per cent increase in the price of grain, citing as their reason the effect of the devaluation on their input costs. The hefty increase of 25 per cent meant starvation or near starvation for the bulk of Zimbabwe's population. This explains why, when the workers' union, the Zimbabwe Congress of Trade Unions (ZCTU), decided to take up the issue of food prices, it had a groundswell of popular support from the bulk of the now impoverished and hard-pressed population. Over the years, especially since 1990, the formal sector workers, like most of the population, have been impoverished. The policy of liberalisation, forced on the government by the IMF, World Bank and the donors as the price for their capital, also affected its role in regulating industrial relations.

Furthermore, the state could no longer play a mediating role between the workers and the employers. It was now free play for collective bargaining, the workers and employers facing one another eyeball to eyeball. Collective bargaining during 1997 was one of the most difficult over the years. (I was personally involved on the workers' side during these negotiations.) The employers claimed that wage increases would render them uncompetitive in the export market, thus defeating one of the purposes of ESAP. At the same time, workers said that they no longer had stomachs over which to tighten the proverbial belt. In a series of wildcat strikes between May and August, the workers were able to secure, on average, a 25 per cent increase over their wages, barely enough to compensate for the raging inflation. The ZCTU called for a nationwide strike to protest against the government tax package. The ZCTU secretary-general, Morgan Tsvangirai, announced that whilst the union was not opposed to the claims of the war veterans, the money should not come out of taxing the already hard-pressed workers. However, this did not sit well with the war veterans, who believed that workers were now about to sabotage their payouts before Christmas. This created conflict between the unions and ex-combatants. In other words, the ordinary people were now divided. On the day of the national mass strike led by the ZCTU on 9 December, people whom the media reported were sent by the War Veterans Association grievously assaulted Morgan Tsvangirai in his office.

Direct action by the landless and land poor peasants and farm workers in June 1997 finally pushed a foot-dragging government into action on land reform. In October, the state announced compulsory land acquisition of 1,471 farms. The Commercial Farmers Union (CFU) announced that if their farms were 'seized', the country would suffer terrible losses amounting to: Z\$5.2 billion in crops; Z\$4 billion in exports of tobacco, beef and cotton; and a drop in employment from 327,000 to 180,000. A visiting UK minister announced that the UK had no obligation to fund land reform, and the IMF suggested that this would send the wrong signals to future investors in Zimbabwe. Several efforts were subsequently made, with the mediation of the UNDP, to bring together the government and the donors and other stakeholders for a systematic resolution of the question. These efforts failed, mainly on account of a hard-line position taken by the British government.

That sealed Zimbabwe's fate for the next ten years. With the people divided between the workers and the war veterans, the government paralysed by the political crisis and unable to see how to bring back the economy to life, and the donors bent on sanctions unless the country was brought back to what they saw as order, the country was torn apart for the next ten years.

Other cases

The perils of Red Aid are not confined to Africa; they are a widespread phenomenon in the developing countries whose governments, either through ignorance or through misplaced goodwill, have allowed themselves to become dependent on donor aid and advice from the IMF and the World Bank for their development strategies.

Mexico 1994–95

In December 1994, Mexico faced a payments crisis, and there was a run on the Mexican peso. The IMF and the United States intervened with approximately US$40 billion to shore up the currency. Who were they protecting? Not the Mexicans as it turned out. The Mexicans paid a heavy price for the bale out. The fall in the peso meant that Mexican assets were devalued in the world market. American and other foreign capital owners picked up these assets at less than a third or a quarter of their original value. The result was that the Mexican middle class found the assets that they owned were hollowed out. Almost overnight a section of the middle class was wiped out. Furthermore, they had to hand over national control of oil to the American banks, which became the receivers of the oil revenue in order to pay out the foreign creditors, mostly the banks themselves. The Mexicans had jealously guarded their sovereignty over oil for decades, but in one fell swoop, almost overnight and because of the peso crisis, they were forced to surrender their national patrimony to foreign control as the price for being 'baled out'. Mexicans were compelled by the terms of the bail-out to open up and accept joint ventures with foreign capitalists. The 'tequila factor' reverberated disconcertingly for several months in the region. Since 1995, Mexico has further liberalised its trade and investment regimes. It is now facing massive deindustrialisation and joblessness.

East Asian crisis 1997–98

In the 1990s, the Thai government had liberalised capital flows partly as a result of pressure from the IMF. Much of the funds came through the banking system on short call (ranging from overnight calls to six months duration), and were lent long to private sector enterprises. The value of the collaterals offered by the private sector turned out to be extremely questionable because they were largely based on inflated property prices. So when the crunch came, following a speculative run on the baht in August 1997, the foreign investors panicked and started withdrawing their funds from Thailand. As a result, the banks began calling back their loans, and of course the private sector could not repay them: they defaulted. In trying to shore up the baht, the central bank depleted most of the country's reserves. In the follow-up, many of the banks were liquidated, or consolidated, and the state decided to take over the burden of repaying the loans. In other words, *private debts were transformed into public debts*. Soon the Thai crisis rippled across to Indonesia, the Philippines, Malaysia and Korea. According to the *The Economist*:

> For much of the region, the crisis destroyed wealth on a massive scale and sent absolute poverty shooting up. In the banking system alone, corporate loans equivalent to around half of one year's GDP went bad – a destruction of savings on a scale more usually associated with a full-scale war.[5]

In the follow-up, the medicine offered by the IMF was worse than the disease. The governments of many of these countries (unwisely) accepted IMF advice to raise interest rates and other austerity measures. They also agreed to further open up their economies. This did not result in more capital inflow, as the IMF had envisaged. Instead, the economies plunged, and governments had to sell national assets (including banks) in order to stabilise their currency and the economy.

The social and political consequences of these actions

deepened the crisis. In Indonesia, the anger and frustration of the general population was targeted against the government. Their immediate demand was for *reformasi* and an end to corrupt and military-backed governments. In Korea, thousands of workers took to the streets in protest against IMF austerity measures and the subsequent retrenchments. South Korea was forced to sell several national assets to foreigners, mostly Americans and Japanese, at well below their real worth. But the US trounced Japan in this game. The IMF poured $120 billion into South Korea, Thailand and Indonesia, but, under pressure from the United States, subverted Japan's offer of a $100 billion fund to buffer Asian currencies.

Only in Malaysia, did things go differently. The maverick Mahathir reinstated national controls over capital movements, and pegged foreign exchange and interest rates.[6]

Argentina 2001

Argentina has long been modelled by IMF and World Bank experts as the paragon of the Washington consensus, an exemplary country that abolished trade barriers, opened itself up to the free inflow and outflow of capital, tied its currency to the US dollar, and privatised practically everything, from banks to malls, to attract foreign direct investment. In December 2001 the model collapsed like a pack of cards. The country simply disintegrated in a morass of economic, social and political chaos following the default on $155 billion of debt (the largest in history).

As had happened after the earlier Mexican crisis and the East Asian crisis, the IMF experts first washed their hands of any responsibility for the collapse of Argentina,[7] and then began to find *post facto* explanations for yet another 'surprise' event. Each expert had their own theory for the collapse, but they were unanimous in pinning the blame on the government of Argentina for bad management of the economy. The issue to question was not the IMF-inspired strategy, they argued, but its implementation – such as keeping a fixed exchange rate for too long, lax fiscal policy, relying on foreign borrowing to fund profligate government spending, not disciplining provincial government spending, and so on.

In all this postmortem what was lost sight of was the plight of ordinary citizens, who could not even access their bank accounts in order to draw out money to meet weekly expenses. A country, whose income per capita was almost on par with that of France, Germany and Canada in the 1930s, and whose workers had given to the world the famous ballroom dance the tango, became overnight 'just another third world country'. The middle classes simply disintegrated, except those that were unpatriotic enough to have externalised their savings in the US before the foredoomed collapse.

Africa

Africa was worst hit by IMF and World Bank Red Aid conditionalities. To be sure, the earlier phases of industrialisation (the import substitution phase of the 1960s and 1970s, and the state-subsidised, export-oriented phase of the 1980s and 1990s) gave birth to cost-inefficient industries in Africa, often at the cost of agriculture. They also added to the increasing balance of payments problems on top of the already heavy external debts that most countries had to service. Nonetheless, those early phases did create a certain industrial infrastructure in many parts of Africa, and spin-offs in technological and managerial skills. During the 1980s and 1990s, most of the countries that came under the austerity and export-led strategies of the IMF and World Bank became hostages to the demands of liberalisation and privatisation. Under the so-called Washington consensus, state-controlled industries were systematically dismantled everywhere in Africa; some of these industries were actually closed down, whilst others were bought up by foreign corporations. Trade liberalisation, on the other hand opened the door to cheaper imports from outside, and many of the cost-inefficient African industries were shut down in the face of increased competition. Instead of making them 'more efficient' in the heat of competition, they simply shut down and set thousands of workers onto the streets.

Conclusion and postscript

It is clear that IMF bail-outs to the hard-pressed economies of all these countries in the South that, through ignorance or naivety, accepted them, were not to protect these economies. The objective, or at any rate the effect, was to bail out hard-pressed American financial and banking interests, and to create conditions for further control by American (and allied) capital over the national economies of the developing countries in distress. In other words, these developing countries were placed in distress through debt burden, trade liberalisation, and the other Red Aid conditionalities of donor funding, and then to get them out of the distress, the IMF moved in and cleared the way for American-European-Japanese capital to take over. This, at least, is what evidence shows on the ground, whatever the neoliberal theorists might say in their erudite books.[8]

Larry Summers, the intellectual power behind US foreign policy in economic affairs and more of a practitioner than a theorist, said: 'In some ways the IMF has done more in these past months to liberalise these economies and open their markets to US goods and services than has been achieved in rounds of trade negotiations in the region.'[9]

Even the London-based *The Economist* had to admit that the IMF's Korea foray proved that it has become an 'adjunct to US foreign policy'.[10] In Korea, the IMF is seen, *The Economist* added, not as rescuer but as tool of US and Japanese colonialism.[11] It went on to say that the USA also had a 'big hand' in dictating IMF conditions for baling out Mexico and Indonesia.[12] In the IMF, *The Economist* concluded, it is 'politics in command'.

In February 2000, the US Congressional Meltzer Commission reported that the IMF and the World Bank were victims of 'mission creep'. The IMF, first conceived as a provider of liquidity in emergencies, had become a development institution, advising and requiring borrowers not merely to repay, but to reform the deep microstructure of their economies. It had little expertise in this area. The World Bank, on the other hand, had not broadened its operations; rather, it had failed to narrow them as conditions – notably, the development of global financial markets – had changed. Most of its loans went to countries with access to private international capital. The countries which, according to the bank's own analysis, could make best use of its resources received a comparatively small share. To be more effective, the commission concluded, the fund and the bank both needed to do less.

In response to this, Larry Summers advised the US government not to adopt the recommendations of the Meltzer Commission. If adopted, he said, the IMF would cease to serve American interests.[13]

Notes

1 For the following figures, see: United Nations Development Programme (UNDP) (1999) *Zimbabwe Human Development Report.*

2 Government of Zimbabwe (1991) *Zimbabwe: A Framework for Economic Reform 1991–95.*

3 Moyo, T. (1999) 'Financial implications of globalisation', paper prepared for the Poverty Forum, Harare, November.

4 UNDP (1999), p. 63, Table 6.4.

5 *The Economist* (2003) 8 February.

6 Article by Khor, Martin (2005) 'The Malaysian experience in financial-economic crisis management – An alternative to the IMF-style approach', *Third World Network Global Economy Series*, no. 6.

7 Weisbrot, Mark (2001) 'How the IMF messed up Argentina', *International Herald Tribune*, 26 December. See also, Torres, Hector R. (2005) 'Argentina and the IMF: learning lessons from our experience', New York, Initiative for Policy Dialogue, Columbia University.

8 For additional on-the-ground evidence of the effects of SAPs on the economies of Bangladesh, Ecuador, El Salvador, Ghana, Hungary, Mexico, the Philippines, Uganda and Zimbabwe, see SAPRIN (2004) *Structural Adjustment: The Policy Roots of Economic Crisis, Poverty and Inequality*, Zed Books.

9 Summers, Larry (1998) *American Farmers: Their Stakes in Asia, Their Stake in IMF*, Washington DC, Office of Public Affairs, US Treasury Department.

10 *The Economist* (1997) 13 December, p. 80.

11 Ibid, p. 14.

12 Ibid, p. 80.

13 *Wall Street Journal* (2000) Europe, 15 June.

CHAPTER 3

AN EXIT STRATEGY
Seven steps to end aid dependence

Introduction

This monograph is not about countries that have already moved out of aid dependence. It is about largely the hundred or so countries that are classified as the least developed countries (LDCs), the middle-income countries that are not LDCs but that are still struggling to become economically independent from foreign aid, and the vulnerable small and island economies.

A significant point of departure is that we are now living in a different period of history, a period of globalisation where the dictates of global capital, globalised corporations and global institutions (such as the World Bank and the IMF) do not allow much of the domestic policy space that countries such as Korea and Taiwan enjoyed during the Cold War period. We live in a knowledge-intensive economic era, where the knowledge which is embedded in technology is jealously protected by sanctions-bearing intellectual property regimes. So today, developing countries are in a much more difficult era than ever before. For these countries the exit strategy from aid dependence requires a radical shift both in mindset, and a deeper and direct involvement of people in their own development for a more self-reliant economy. For countries in Africa that have emerged from colonial or racial oppression since only the 1960s (in the case of South Africa since only 1994), it would not be an exaggeration to say that they need to prepare for yet another war of liberation.

At the international level, the new situation demands a complete overhaul of the institutions of global governance, including also a radical restructuring of the institutional aid architecture – a shift away from Red and Orange Aids to international assistance of the Green/Blue and Purple hues.

The national project

What is the national project? Against the background of globalisation, some might see the national project as reverting to historical passion and sentimentality. That is not so. It is a serious practical and contemporary issue. The developing countries are in constant battle in the World Trade Organisation (WTO), the World Intellectual Property Organisation (WIPO), the United Nations Conference on Trade and Development (UNCTAD) and other UN agencies to try and defend their policy space against the forces of globalisation and trade and financial liberalisation. To give just but one example: in the WTO, the developing countries have succeeded (so far) in resisting pressure from the developed countries to negotiate the four so-called Singapore issues – competition policy, investment policy, government procurement, and trade facilitation. They have finally agreed on trade facilitation, but remain firm on the first three issues. At least in the multilateral negotiating forums, they are jealously guarding their right to determine policy (national space) in these three areas.

The national project, however, is not solely a nationalist strategy, but a strategy for local, national, regional and South–South self determination, independence, dignity and solidarity. It is the essential political basis for any strategies to end aid dependence. The national project is the continuation of the struggle for independence. It is a project that began before countries in the South got their independence from colonial rule, continued for several decades after political independence, and then, in the era of globalisation, it appeared to have died a sudden death. If it has died, it needs to be revived.

In the case of Africa and Asia, and up to the time of independence, the objective was clear and simple: it was to secure liberation from foreign domination. It was captured by the slogan of the time – self-determination. After independence, however, matters became complicated. People who fought and won independence, involving huge sacrifices (as in, for example, India, Indonesia and Kenya), and in some cases armed action and guerrilla struggles (as in, for example, Algeria, Zimbabwe, Angola and South Africa), began to ask their political leaders and intellectuals some critical questions: Where do we go from here? What now? What do we do with this hard won independence? There also came to the surface even more difficult questions about self-identity that had been subdued during the struggle for independence: Who are we as a 'nation'? How do we forge nationhood out of disparate ethnic, racial, religious, linguistic, regional and sub-regional groupings? Countries in Latin America, who have enjoyed legal independence much longer than those in Asia and Africa, are also facing the same challenges. They are, as the Latinos are fond of saying, 'too far from God and too close to the United States'. Also, in more recent times, the indigenous peoples are beginning to find a voice in the political arena, and are raising questions of identity and participation.

The international dimension of the national project

United by a similar experience of exploitation and national oppression, the erstwhile colonies had a common cause, and some common matters to address at the international level in the years immediately after the Second World War. Three of these were significant:

- The question of their relationship with the former imperial power
- The question of their relations with each other
- The question of how they were to position themselves in the emerging Cold War between the Western bloc and the Soviet bloc.

The first set of answers to these questions was given when, in 1954, India and China formulated five basic principles (called the Panchsheel) that would guide their relations:

- Mutual respect for each other's territorial integrity and sovereignty
- Mutual non-aggression
- Mutual non-interference in domestic affairs
- Equality and mutual benefit
- Peaceful co-existence.

In 1955, the leading lights of the independence struggle – among them, Nehru of India, Nkrumah of Ghana, Nasser of Egypt, Sukarno of Indonesia and Tito of Yugoslavia – met in the Indonesian capital of Bandung. It was a milestone meeting for this is where the so-called Non-Aligned Movement (NAM) was formally founded. Members made a declaration that their countries were not formally aligned with or against any major power blocs; in other words, they were not involved in the Cold War. They also adopted a 'declaration on promotion of world peace and cooperation', which included the five principles, the Panchsheel.

Like all principles and guidelines, the Panchsheel were not always easy to follow; nor, indeed, was the commitment to non-alignment. There were also stresses and strains among these countries (such as in the case of India and Pakistan). Short-term considerations or sheer desperation often drove some of them to solicit help from either one bloc or the other. Furthermore, the two blocs offered divergent paths to development – the capitalist and the socialist roads – and this often created ideological divisions not only between but also within countries. All this was extremely complex, and no simple yardstick (ideological or power political) could measure the conformity or divergence of each country's behaviour from the principles of either non-alignment or the Panchsheel.

Why narrate this familiar story in a book on aid? Because, the movement described above will continue to provide the glue that links the so-called 'third world', or the peoples of the South, as long as the national project is not realised, and as long as aid, or official development assistance (ODA), with all its conditionalities, continues to limit the self-determination of the peoples of the South. The historical experiences are also relevant in the new context of the war on terrorism, and perhaps in future wars related to resource ownership and energy security.

Linking the national and the international aspects of the national project

Indeed, what is remarkable is that despite over half a century of dynamic changes in the global system, including the end of the Cold War, which gave NAM its initial impetus, and despite stresses and tensions within NAM, the movement has retained its underlying relevance and potency to this day. Ever since its first conference in Belgrade in 1961, the members of the movement have met once every few years – for the 14th time in Cuba in September 2006, and for the 15th time in Iran in August 2008. Among the charimen of NAM have been Tito, Nasser, Kaunda, Boumédienne, Fidel Castro, Robert Mugabe, Nelson Mandela, Thabo Mbeki, Mahathir bin Mohammad and Ahmadinejad.

How does one explain the resilience of NAM? Amid many possible explanations, the one that sounds most plausible is that the NAM members are all united, in their different ways, by the dual quest for national identity (the internal struggle to forge a nation) and self-determination (the refusal to again lose their national independence to foreign control).

The concept of 'neocolonialism' became a familiar idiom in political discourse when Kwame Nkrumah popularised it in the 1960s, but its reality predated its popularity. The newly independent countries discovered that they had won political independence, but they still had a long way to go to achieve economic liberation from external ownership and control over their resources and instruments and technology of production. They were also engaged in a global trade and financial relationship that tied them to an unequal exchange with the West. The search for an independent path to development was behind the formation of the Group of 77 and China, and the United Nations Conference on Trade and Development (UNCTAD) in 1964. In the 1970s and 1980s the G77 sought to create a New International Economic Order (NIEO), and a New International Information Order (NIIO), but in the face of relentless opposition from the West, these ideas remained only on the drawing board (though not yet quite dead).

To this day, when the Group of 77 and China talk about 'policy space' in the context of, for example the trade negotiations in the World Trade Organisation (WTO), they refer essentially to the continuing search for independence from the domination of the existing global power holders. The Cold War has ended, but the hegemony of 'the triumphant West' has become, if anything, even more potent. The institutions of global economic governance, put in place over fifty years ago, continue to stretch a long shadow over the developing countries' margins of policy space; longer and darker shadows in the case of some (as in most of Africa) than others.

Therefore, although many have challenged the continued relevance of the NAM, as well as of the G77 and China, especially since the end of the Cold War, it is the guiding principles of these entities that continue to echo the sentiments of most of their respective members (there is a significant overlap in the membership of the G77 and NAM) in their wish for collective action. The purpose of NAM was restated in the Havana Declaration of 1979. It is to ensure 'the national independence, sovereignty, territorial integrity and security of non-aligned countries' in their 'struggle against imperialism, colonialism, neo-colonialism, racism, Zionism, and all forms of foreign aggression, occupation, domination, interference or hegemony as well as against great power and bloc politics.'

Thirty years down the road since Havana, the countries of the South are still struggling to gain control over their policy space.

Demise and revival in the 1980s and 1990s

Since the mid-1980s, however, the developing countries have faced serious challenges:

- In the 1980s, the rise of neoliberal globalisation and the emergence of a unipolar power and its allies, with their domineering control over global institutions
- In the 1990s and beyond, the predominance of speculative capital over productive capital
- In the 2001 and beyond, the startling reality of wars fought by developed countries against or in countries in Asia, Latin America and Africa in the name of fighting terrorism
- In 2007–08 and beyond, the challenges posed by rising energy and food prices.

To elaborate on all these would require hundreds of pages. A brief description may suffice in order to put aid into its proper political-economic context.

It is difficult to give an exact date, but the impulse behind neoliberal globalisation came with multipronged crises faced by the developed countries following oil, finance and food crises in the beginning of the 1970s, saturation of Western markets in investment finance and goods, the fall of the Shah of Iran in 1979, the invasion of Afghanistan in the same year, the domestic crisis of profitability, the rising demand of the working classes (especially in the UK) for a better share in the national income, and the looming recession. First Thatcher in the UK and then Reagan in the US responded to these multifaceted crises by deregulating the economy, privatising national assets, imposing firm control over the workers (through, for example, introducing labour flexibility), and trade and financial liberalisation. Later, in the form of the so-called Washington consensus, it was to dominate the thinking of the Bretton Woods institutions and the WTO.

The devastating effects of the neoliberal credo on many

countries of the South materialised in the form of Red Aid, as described above. The effects of the predominance of speculative capital over productive capital in the 1990s and beyond manifested themselves as financial crises in Mexico, East Asia and Argentina (also Russia, although not described above). The third phenomenon that merits close analysis is the post 9/11 scenario, in which the only remaining super power seized the opportunity to launch two pre-emptive wars against Afghanistan and Iraq together with its 'coalition of the willing', with a new rationale and justification for intervening in the so-called axis of evil and failed states. Finally, in more recent years, we are witnessing the looming struggle for resources (especially energy and food), and the battle over climate change.

It is necessary to add that these four crises are not simply sequential challenges. They have not just come one after the other. They have come one on top of the other. It is like having a deck of cards put on top of a second deck, and a third on top of the first two. Instead of having to tackle one challenge, the countries of Asia, Latin America, and Africa have to tackle four challenges, all at the same time.

The revival of the national project

Through all these challenges, the national project and the determination to stick together as 'the South' have not only survived but are now witnessing a revival. The geo-economic landscape has altered fundamentally in the last decade. Some countries in the South, although still developing countries, have become global players in trade and investment finance, and are able to insulate themselves (at least partially) from the effects of economic recession in the North, which they would have been unable to do less than a decade ago. The rising price of oil has put wealth in the hands of oil-producing countries in the South that today know better than they did in previous oil booms how to use this bonanza for national and regional development – for example in the Gulf region, and in Southern America.

Non-alignment of the earlier era had an *activist* as well as a *rejectionist* side to it. What was rejected was involvement in the conflict between the Western capitalist world and the Eastern communist world. The activist side was the affirmation of the five Bandung principles that embodied aspirations towards peaceful co-existence, and non-interference in the internal affairs of each other; the struggle for liberation from colonialism and racism; the successful creation of UNCTAD; and the attempt at creating a NEIO.

In our own time, the NAM and G77 also have both a rejectionist aspect and an activist one.

On the rejection front, these principles are the:

- Rejection of war as an instrument of policy, and of the doctrine of preventive or pre-emptive war
- Rejection of extra-territorial jurisdiction of the hegemons, including the doctrine of humanitarian intervention or the newly coined phrase – 'responsibility to protect' – as a pretext to justify hegemonic intervention in the affairs of the countries of the third world
- Rejection of double standards in which, for example, the countries of the third world must practice free trade while the hegemonic states practice protectionism
- Rejection of unilateralism on the part of the superpower hegemon
- Rejection of the Washington consensus, the one-size-fits-all formula and the unfettered domination of the WTO and the Bretton Woods institutions.
- Rejection of the notion that the market is the arbiter of all human values and a fair distributor of wealth. In this respect, therefore, rejection of the practices that turn nature and the environment, as well as vulnerable sections of society – including the labour and dignity of women, children, minorities, and refugees – into marketable commodities

- Rejection of the domination of a few hundred global transnational corporations that control the world's finances, natural resources, research and technology, production, and distribution outlets
- Rejection of policies that undermine or subvert the South's policy options
- Rejection of invitations to join 'coalitions of the willing' created by the hegemonic powers to give their interventionist policies third world legitimacy, and the corollary that countries are either with the hegemonic powers or against them
- Rejection of the notion that governments of the third world need to be isolated, punished and placed under sanctions if they do not follow the ideologies and values imposed on them.

On the positive, activist front, the principles are:

- Respect for international law, though there are aspects of it that may need review in view of the demands of the present times
- Support to strengthen the United Nations, though there are also aspects of the organisation (for example, the composition and powers of the Security Council) that need to be reviewed in the light of contemporary exigencies and power realities
- Support for the internationally agreed development goals (IADGs) including the Millennium Development Declaration and the Millennium Development Goals (MDGs), although it is becoming apparent that they deal with only symptoms, and that the policies of the developed countries and the present structures of global governance will make it difficult to achieve these goals
- An alternative policy on innovation, science and technology, based on sharing of technology and know-how, and harnessing the collective knowledge and wisdom of the people

- A people-led and home-grown (as opposed to the Bretton Woods institutions and donor-led) development strategy
- At the regional and bi-regional levels, grassroots-led regional integration (as opposed to the Western countries-led vertical and imbalanced integration). In this respect the promotion of the Global System of Trade Preferences between countries of the South in a system of trade preferences where trade concessions are linked to the level of development, and concessions made in a South–South context do not have to be extended to the developed countries
- At the national economic level, an alternative production system, one that is based on domestic demand and human needs, and the use of local resources and domestic savings and labour. This should lead to the horizontal integration of agriculture and industry (as opposed to the inherited vertical integration of each sector separately with the economies of the empire), and increasing (rather than as at present diminishing) returns to labour
- A pro-active strategy of protecting and nurturing the environment and the global and national natural resource consistent with the imperatives of development and justice.

The above provides the overarching global and historically evolving setting to the NAM's 'national' expression at the country level, down to the psychological mind set of individual leaders and the ordinary people and the creation of democratic institutions.

What creates aid dependence?

Five principal forces create aid dependence:

1 Past structures of historically embedded relations between the former imperial and colonial powers and

the so-called developing countries. These structures are reinforced by aid, among other tools of Northern control, including the Bretton Woods institutions, and the ideology of market fundamentalism, including its current incarnation, neoliberal globalisation.

2   Lack of availability of alternatives to aid dependence, reinforced by pressing needs to solicit aid for, among other things, balancing the budget, restoring balance of payments problems, purchasing machinery and equipment tied to aid, humanitarian causes, natural catastrophes, etc.

3   Aid as a soft option. Looking for domestic resources for development is too much hard work, and creates domestic enemies, when there are always donors around who can provide the necessary funds if their bidding is done on commercial, political and military matters

4   A psychology of aid dependence among the peoples of the South, reinforced by a lack of self-confidence in their own ability, inadequate feelings of responsibility for self and national development, and a lack of courage to displease the donors by failing to show gratitude for their generosity. Disillusioned with the policies and corruption of their leaders, the ordinary people are sometimes even more inclined to seek outside assistance to get them out of their current predicament.

5   Third world governments who do not accept aid are often made to feel (by the donors, by the media, and by their own citizens) that they are being irresponsible about the plight of the poor, which they believe only donor aid can adequately address.

There are other factors that create, or reinforce, aid dependence such as a lack vision among the political leadership in many countries of the South, ever ready for a photo opportunity to shake hands with the presidents and prime ministers of the big Western powers. But these five are the principal causes of aid dependence.

Seven steps to end aid dependence

Step 1: Adjusting the mindset

Ending aid dependence is not a one-day project. Deeply embedded structures and the power of vested interests do not disappear overnight. Neither do they disappear on their own. Cutting off from aid dependence is an act of political will. Aid's demise has to be strategised carefully, like fighting a war, no less. It cannot be left only to politicians, or officials, or experts. However, without their active involvement the strategy cannot succeed. It is the combined efforts of the people and their leaders that can lift the mental shackles of the past.

Whatever the challenges, the first place to start is the mind, the psychology of dependence, fostered and fed by lengthy relationships with the donors. It can begin with individuals (even a single individual), but nationally a critical mass has to develop before it can acquire political force and institutional expression. Institutionally, it can begin with circles of citizenry collectively thinking and brainstorming about the best way to get out of the trap of aid dependence, the circles getting bigger and bigger until the new mindset becomes part of the 'national ethos', and part of the national mandate cutting across political parties, social groups, and age and gender divides. Symbolically, and politically, the next step would be reached when a critical mass of the members of local assemblies and the national parliament would say: 'We have had enough of this dependence on aid. We resolve to end it and become self-reliant. Development is our responsibility, and not that of the donors.'

This is the first step, the first and biggest hurdle to overcome: the will to take the destiny of the nation into one's own hands. This does not mean aid will have no role to play at all, but the psychological liberation from aid dependence is the first step in bringing some clarity to thinking. It is only when people step out of the box that they realise that the nation can begin to clearly think about what kinds of aid might be welcome, which might not, and what role aid could play in the national strategy for endogenous development.

Some people might try and equate endogenous development with autarchy – that dreaded word in free trade circles. However, it must be made clear that endogenous development is not autarchy or isolation from the rest of the world. It is not even 'protectionism'. These are just scare words to trick the mind. Endogenous development, as defined earlier, is simply the beginning of a long democratic process that starts from within, where people participate in the decisions that affect their lives, without imperial interference from outside. It is aimed at improving the lives of the people and the realisation of their potential for self support, free from fear of want and political, economic and social exploitation. As we put it in the earlier formula: Development = $SF + DF - IF$.

Does that mean that there is no place for development aid? No, it does not. It means that before we decide what role aid plays in the development process, we have to understand what development means and what constitutes aid. Aid has to be defined in its proper historical and political context by the people through their own democratic institutions.

Take the case of global public goods (GPGs), for example. It was argued earlier that there are legally binding commitments, such as on climate change and other GPGs. They are part of global obligations undertaken by the developed countries in internationally agreed treaties and conventions. Whether these countries meet these obligations, and how to deal with the situation if they do not, is a matter of law and building global institutions that ensure that they do – a subject to which we come later. But, clearly, in the particular case of climate change, for example, if the developed countries (or the World Bank) attempt to transfer funds as loans that are expected to be repaid (with interest), then that would be a violation of the premise on which the Climate Investment Fund is created.

This matter will be taken up later. However, a subject that cannot be discussed in any detail in this monograph is the issue of investments and the role that foreign direct investments (FDIs) play (or can play) in development. Here the focus is on the issue of aid, and the point made repeatedly is that aid dependence is not the route to go for promoting endogenous development. The role of foreign investments should be treated just as carefully as aid.

The leap from the neoliberal to endogenous development is fraught with many challenges. But the first challenge is in the mind. If you cannot conceive self-determination of the destiny of your own nation, then you allow yourself to be determined by external forces. The opposite of self-determination is donor-determination.

Step 2 Budgeting for the poor not for the donors

Whilst the psychological leap from aid dependence to aid exit is gathering momentum, groups of citizens might already begin to work on the essential task of budgeting for the poor as opposed to budgeting for the donors.

Valuable conceptual and methodological lessons can be learnt from the experience of women's organisations that have examined their nations' budgets through the gender lens. It is surprising how male-gendered most national budgets are, and not only in the developing countries. In those African countries in which I have mainly worked, I have often come across budgets for the agricultural sector, for instance, in which it was always assumed that land should be (as of right, as it were) owned by men, and that all extension agricultural experts should be men, although the bulk of the cultivators are actually women.

Traditional budget planning

It is the same with the traditional methodology of preparing national budgets. They are prepared to please outsiders rather than the people. The top–down bureaucratic minds that craft national budgets in many developing countries usually ask the following five 'planning' questions:

1 What kind of 'enabling environment' should we create internally in order to entice foreign capital to come and help with our development?

2 Within that enabling environment framework, how much room is there for national priorities, especially for maintaining internal law and order (police, prisons and the judiciary), defence and foreign policy (the army, ministry of foreign affairs, etc), and social services (health, education, etc)? A donor-savvy, skilled budget planner can find ways of shifting some of the burdens of defence, internal order and health and education to the 'donor basket'.

3 Who are the key donors that should be consulted in the process?

4 Within the overall planned expenditure for the next year, or three or five years, how much can be raised by way of internal taxation and tariff revenue (what, in the language of the Monterrey Consensus, is called 'domestic resource mobilisation')?

5 How can all this be packaged to look like budgeting for the poor – as a strategy for poverty reduction, which is what donors require in order to legitimise their largesse as development aid?

For brevity of reference let us put this along a cascading continuum:

1 Enabling environment for foreign capital and aid

2 Building national priorities into the donor basket

3 Key donors to consult

4 Domestic resource mobilisation

5 Packaging for the poor

Let us discuss the last first, because it is the fig leaf that covers the bare essentials, for without it the nudity of the planning process could become all too apparent. In the 1980s and 1990s, for example, the World Bank devised a fairly elaborate system of what was called the ESAPs and later the PRSPs – Poverty Reduction Strategy Papers. The whole process of planning was top–down. Once this was completed, civil society (in those days called non-governmental organisations) were invited to make their input. This was called participatory planning. Many of these NGOs were also funded by the donors. The NGOs were supposed to represent the people. They were a substitute for the people. Once the World Bank had involved the NGOs, it could say, 'The people were consulted; we have embarked on a people-driven process.' Once the fig leaf was in place, the implementation of the budget (including getting it approved by the parliament) and resource mobilisation (internal and external) could now proceed as planned. This is not just a caricature of reality; it is reality exposed, without flesh and feathers, to its bare bones.

A close examination of the national budgets of many developing countries would surprise even the most critical of observers at how these are crafted with the donor countries in mind. In many African countries the World Bank and the donors sit in on every planning meeting from the beginning to the end, involving NGOs and parliament only towards the end to endorse what has already been agreed between state bureaucrats and the donors. This is true, strangely, even in those African countries that fought for their independence from the West through bitter guerrilla warfare.

In Zimbabwe, for example, following decades of bitter guerrilla war, its post-independence government was lured by the promise of development aid, so one of the first things it did was to call a donors' conference. Next door, in South Africa, in the spirit of self-reliance and people-oriented thinking, the government produced a well thought-through programme of self-development called the Restoration Development Programme. It was home-grown, i.e. not inspired by the World Bank or the IMF. In June 1994, however, this was replaced by GEAR – the Growth, Employment, and Redistribution programme, apparently in consultation with the World Bank and the IMF. It was a neoliberal inspired agenda that, the government hoped, would attract donors and investors from abroad. The government also committed itself to paying all the odious debts incurred by past regimes against which it had struggled and sacrificed for decades, in the hope that the country would then receive a triple-A rating from Western agencies, and thus attract foreign capital.

Budgeting for the poor

Budgeting for the poor is a different kind of exercise. Indeed, the word 'for' is already misplaced. The budgeting is done not with the poor 'in the minds of the experts'; it is done by the poor them-selves, from bottom–up. Of course, the 'poor' is a loose term: how poor do you have to be before you are defined as poor?[1]

However, in the context of planning, it means that budgeting starts at the lowest level of social and productive organisation, say the village level. Of course, the village cannot plan for matters at the macro level – things like defence of the nation, foreign policy, exchange rate policy, etc. That is understood. These are broader matters of state and economy that require a more sophisticated approach. Here we get into the complex question of the interac-tion between the village and the nation as intermediated by the people's elected representatives (the parliament), the role of politi-cal parties, the role of political leadership, the importance of peo-ple's conscientisation about matters of state and foreign policy, the role of mass media and mass education, and so on. In Cuba, for example, Fidel Castro used to spend long hours talking directly to the people, explaining the basis and the reasoning behind difficult foreign policy or security matters, and even explaining the complexities of, for example, foreign exchange and petrol rationing.

Then again, it is not really true that ordinary people cannot understand larger issues of national policy. In Bolivia, for example, people who have been impoverished through centuries by foreign corporations' exploitation of their natural gas resources finally came out against it, and put one of themselves, Evo Morales, in power. In Uganda, small farmers have come out against the Economic Partnership Agreements with the European Union.

Those who are attuned to thinking in the traditional way of planning (with donor assistance) may be turned off by the above references to Brazil, Cuba, Bolivia or Venezuela. It is part of the mindset created by the media and the donors that potrays Cuba as a communist country, where the people have no freedom, and where the regime denies people access to consumer goods they dearly want, such as private cars and holidays abroad. What is seldom communicated by the efficiency oriented donors and the media is that Cuba scores highly in UNDP's Human Development Index.[2] Cuba's strategy fits with the formula of development as social factor plus democratic factor minus imperial factor (Development = SF + DF – IF). Most developing countries strategy follows the neoliberal formula: Development = Growth + Wealth accumulation + Trickle down to the poor.

If Cuba is too extreme an example, as some readers may argue, then let us look at less extreme examples, and the lessons that can be learnt from these. One does not have to completely emulate Cuba's revolution (in spite of the appeal of the emblematic figure Che Guevara) because, of course, every situation is different.

In India, for example, The Citizen's Forum (comprising well known grassroots organisations and individuals) made a critique of the UPA Budget for 2004–05. Its essential message was that 'the

3 per cent cannot ignore the 97 per cent'. The budget, it argued, was 'not transparently drafted'. Of the agricultural sector it said:

> The budget is supposed to be a pro Agriculture budget but we find that it is focused on Agri-Business and the rich farmers instead of the small and marginal farmers and the landless labourers in rural India. This emphasis needs to be changed. Agro processing needs to be promoted in a decentralised manner (not corporatised). Cooperative sector needs to be promoted along milk-producers cooperative model of the Anand Milk Union Limited (AMUL) and not Corporate model. To check distress amongst farmers (resulting in suicides) cost of inputs need to be controlled, procurement should be strengthened and false propaganda regarding high incomes from new high cost crops should be made illegal. Agricultural research needs to focus on the small farms.[3]

In Brazil in the Province of Rio Grande do Sul, Partnership Budget Planning used new models for urban planning. Municipalities formed counter models to carry out diagnostic analysis, expose social injustice, redefine the role of the public service, mobilise local actors, and correct the 'mistakes' of centralised state planning. They worked on some basic principles including, for example, democratisation of decision making through direct citizen participation, development of civic consciousness, accountability for all expenditure and investments, and an education pedagogy that fosters solidarity, cooperation, sharing, and protection of minorities (as opposed to one that fosters egoism, greed, competition and accumulation).

Such experiments in people's budget planning, it must be added, are not confined to developing countries. In Canada, for example, citizen groups in several provinces have been doing this for years.

Many of these experiments are still in their early stages, or are not allowed to mature by more powerful social and political forces at the national and local (as well as global) levels, who perceive these attempts as threats to their monopolistic interests and power over decision making, and they manage to reverse the processes of people power. Often the local or community level experiments have little impact at the national level because they are atomised with little contact with one another. And so, many of these experiments get neutralised or marginalised and fail to scale up. Nonetheless, what is significant about these is that, despite setbacks and the many challenges these experiments face, they demonstrate what is possible and doable, and constitute the reservoir for alternative solutions.

Step 3 Putting employment and decent wages upfront

Declining share of returns to labour

The labour force is one of the most important productive resources. There is, however, an imbalance between the returns to the labour force and the rate of capital accumulation as well as the technological progress. In his Report to the 2007 International Labour Organisation (ILO) Conference, Director General Juan Somavia gave some interesting figures.[4] For 16 industrialised countries, employee compensation (wages plus employers' social security contributions) declined from 58 to around 55 per cent of GDP between 1980 and 2004. If the 'labour' income of the self-employed and other own-account workers is included, the decline in the labour share of national income is steeper, falling from around 68 to 62 per cent. The decline in the labour share of national income is consistent with the perceived shift in the relative market power of labour and capital following the integration of several very populous countries offering low wages into the global economic system and the effects of labour-saving technological change originating in the advanced countries. When national income increasingly goes to the owners of capital rather than to workers, inequality in the distribution of income is likely to increase, since the returns on capital largely accrue to a wealthy minority.[5] This is the global picture, but it hits the developing countries the hardest. (This is consistent with the example we have from Zimbabwe, see pp. 47–57).

Somavia repeated the warning of the World Commission on the Social Dimension of Globalisation that the 'current process of globalisation is generating unbalanced outcomes, both between and within countries ... These global imbalances are morally unacceptable and politically unsustainable.'[6] He added that 'Social inequality within and between nations, exacerbated by the uneven distribution of the benefits and costs of globalisation, is a serious threat to sustainable development';[7] and that 'Market-driven economies, without effective public policies and strong social partners, do not automatically promote social inclusion, nor do they create enough routes to productive and decent work for the disadvantaged.'[8]

In many developing countries, self-employed and casual wage labourers account for at least 60 per cent of the labour force. In its report in January 2008,[9] the ILO gave some figures on what it describes as 'vulnerable employment'. In terms of vulnerable employment as a share of total employment, South Asia, with a rate of 77.2 per cent, was followed by sub-Saharan Africa at 72.9 per cent, South-East Asia and the Pacific at 59.4 per cent, East Asia at 55.7 per cent, Latin America and the Caribbean at 33.2 per cent, the Middle East at 32.2 per cent and North Africa at 30.7 per cent.

LDCs caught in a Malthusian trap

UNCTAD, in its Least Developed Country Report 2006,[10] also had some interesting figures.

- The total labour force of the LDCs was 312 million people in 2000 and is estimated to increase by 89 million to 2010 (total of 401 million people).
- For 36 out of 50 LDCs the labour force is expected to increase by more than 25 per cent.

- As the urbanisation rate has increased (1980: 17 per cent; 2000: 25 per cent) the share of the population engaged in non-agricultural activities has also steadily increased (1980: 21 per cent; 2000: 29 per cent).

The LDCs, the report predicted, will face an increasing challenge to absorb labour productively within agriculture, for three principal reasons:

- Major inequalities in the access to land resources
- Significant share of land holdings are very small
- The yields are low and the level of investment in irrigation and modern inputs (such as fertilisers) is not enough to sustain labour productivity.

The study concludes: 'The combination of little land and low yields means that the poorest farmers are simply too asset-poor to make a good living from farming.'

If agriculture cannot absorb more labour, even less promising are non-agricultural productive employment opportunities to absorb the increasing labour force, mainly on account of the de-industrialisation of these countries' economies following structural adjustment programmes. The UNCTAD study shows that the consequence of this is the rise of the informal sector. Employment in informal sector enterprises constitutes 70–80 per cent of the non-agricultural work force, while it only contributes 40–50 per cent of non-agricultural GDP. The characteristics of informal work are: small survivalist activities, low entry requirements, small scale of operation and rudimentary capital equipment, and basic skills.

Data on Benin, Burkina Faso, Mali and Senegal[11] show that:

- Informal economies are the major source of employment, providing 77 per cent of jobs on average
- On average only about 12 per cent of the labour force are in private formal enterprises in the capital cities
- Average incomes in the informal sector are lower than

those of the private, formal enterprises, which again are lower than those of the public administration and enterprises
- Underemployment and inadequate incomes are major problems in the urban labour markets and are *closely related to lack of formal sector employment.*

What then is the alternative?

The challenge facing the LDCs is to ensure that the growth of the economically active population is associated with *productive labour absorption* in both agriculture and non-agriculture sectors. What is needed, the UNCTAD study concludes, is *structural* change. This means a focus on sustainable agricultural intensification and the creation of productive non-agricultural employment, which will require increased capital accumulation, technological learning and innovation.

It requires bottom–up national development planning so that the aspirations, industriousness and skills of its population from the villages upwards can be built upon. In the case of China, for example, the peasantry has been a source of entrepreneurship and has contributed to the country's success as is evident by the township and village enterprises dotting China. The LDCs need to ensure that their peasantry is protected against the onslaught of policy prescriptions which favour capital-intensive and corporate-driven agribusiness. Protection of the peasantry will be essential to provide food security and maintain sovereignty over national development plans.

Step 4 Creating the domestic market and owning domestic resources

The primacy of the domestic market

The primacy of the domestic over the export market is unassailable in both logic and history. Take the counter logic first, and take the obvious cases – the Gulf States and Botswana. Surely, for them exports must be more important than the domestic market. What will they do with their oil or their diamonds if they do not find an export market? They must surely seek their wealth in exports first before they can put the proceeds of exports into domestic growth.

This is true enough, and there is no point denying its logic. And yet even in these cases, rather exceptional as they are, the creation of a domestic market is essential if they are to generate employment for their people, or for people of their region. The Gulf countries are fast developing their domestic economies based on their oil wealth. They can afford to import most of their consumer needs, but they are building value added domestic assets in other areas such as in transport, communications, tourism and financial services, for without these they would be hostage to the vagaries of the export market. Botswana, too, is adding value to its diamonds by undertaking to polish them at home rather than exporting them in raw form.

Exceptional cases, however, do not make the general rule. In general, all countries have developed by first ensuring that their domestic markets are created, protected and expanded before they have opened them up to foreign competition in return for seeking export markets for their products. The oldest instance of this, of course, is England. It became the world's biggest trading nation only after first becoming its biggest manufacturing nation. For example, through export and export tariffs on unprocessed wool under Henry VII, England created the woollen manufacturing industry. Its slave trade and trade in spices, gold and silver – most of these simply appropriated from foreign lands – were only the means for creating wealth and infrastructure for domestic manufacturing and the domestic market. Countries that followed England on the path to industrialisation – such as Germany, France, Italy and the United States – had first to protect their domestic markets from the more competitively produced English manufactured goods through tariffs and other barriers against imports. Furthermore, they imposed performance requirements on foreign investors to ensure domestic development. All this is well documented in a wonderful little book by Professor Ha-Joon Chang, called *Kicking Away the Ladder: Development Strategy in Historical Perspective*.[12] In an abridged version done for the South Centre, Professor Chang says:

> Virtually all of today's developed countries built up their economies using tariffs and subsidies (and many other measures of government intervention) throughout the 19th century and most of the 20th century (in particular, until the early 1970s). Throughout most of the period between the 1820s and 1945, the United States maintained average industrial tariffs at around 40 per cent, and never below 25 per cent except for brief periods, far higher than those it accepts from the developing countries in the NAMA negotiations today. Five of the six fastest growing developed economies in the so-called 'Golden Age' (1950–73) were high tariff countries (Japan, Italy, Australia, Finland and France).[13]

Flaws of an export-led growth strategy

To return to logic, an export-led development strategy is seriously flawed for many reasons: it distorts development priorities, diverts resources away from the basic needs of the population, creates the wrong kinds of skills, and makes the economy precariously vulnerable to the hazards of international trade and capital movements. One reason why large countries such as India and China are cushioned from the negative effects of the crisis in the Western economies is that they have very large domestic markets. Of course, they are not completely shielded, because with the recession in the US and the West their export earnings will be hurt, but not as much as the countries that are export dependent, especially on the US market, such as Indonesia, Thailand, the Philippines and many countries in Latin America and Africa.

Practical policy implications

Both logic and history demonstrate the wisdom of securing domestic markets. In practical terms, a domestic demand-led strategy means:

- Production of essential food, energy and basic consumer goods
- Ownership of land, sources of water, essential agricultural seeds, natural resources such as minerals, forests, fish reservoirs and stock animals, including farmers' and communities' rights to the genetic resources of their produce[14]
- Tariff protection for these essential products (called 'special products' in the WTO jargon)
- Horizontal linkages between agriculture, industry and services, with domestic value added and virtuous spin-off effects up and down the value chain
- Sufficient wages in the hands of the workers and ordinary consumers so as to pay for essential products and basic services and sustain the domestic market
- Adequate prices for the farmers, especially small farmers, so as to cover the cost of agricultural production, storage and marketing as well as the purchase of food, clothing, shelter and other essential goods
- State provision of basic services, such as health, education and care for the sick and the vulnerable.

This is consistent with the earlier definition of development as comprising social goods, democratic practice, and minimal interference from imperial forces.

Step 5 Plugging the resource gap

One of the reasons advanced by orthodox economists as to why Africa needs aid is that there is a 'savings' or 'resource gap' in Africa. They say Africa's saving rate is very low – 2 to 3 per cent of GNP. Therefore if Africa wants a growth rate of 7 per cent (the New Partnership for Africa's Development, or NEPAD, figure), there has to be an inflow of about 4 to 5 per cent of GNP in the form of either aid or private flows. This argument is also used for other developing countries. On close analysis, it turns out that the orthodox economists' analysis on the savings or resource gap is not empirical but tautological. Let us examine this tautology because its circular logic hides the reality on the ground. I shall make this as simple as possible.

Take the famous equation:

$$Y - E = S \qquad (1)$$

where Y and E are national income and expenditure, and S is national saving. If one wishes to make saving as the focus of one's inquiry, then the equation could be written as:

$$S = Y - E \qquad (2)$$

The equation itself says nothing about any particular reality. It is simply a logical construct. All that it says is that national saving is whatever remains of national income after expenditure.

In order to reach the reality on the ground, one has to look into the actual sources and amounts of national income and the sources and amounts of actual expenditure. A country like Angola, for example, may have a huge income from the sale of its oil and minerals, but most of it could go on two major items of expenditure – war and the profits taken out of the country by foreign companies exploiting the oil. The result could be zero saving or, if the country has to borrow money to finance the war, negative (domestic) savings. Or to make a more general point, part of the expenditure might consist of revenues externalised into foreign banks by a corrupt bureaucracy. So once again, there may be zero or near to zero savings. Or if the country borrows from the external market, then there is negative saving, in other words the country gets into external debt. The equation may thus be written as:

$$Sd = Y - Ed - Ee \qquad (3)$$

where Sd is domestic saving, and Ed and Ee are domestic expenditure and externalised expenditure. The objective here is not to get into conventional GDP calculations. The advantage of the above formula (and its only objective in this monograph) is that it draws attention to externalised expenditure. What is this? Let us give a few examples:

- 'Project fees' (proverbially 10 per cent) paid into the accounts of corrupt politicians and bureaucrats in Swiss banks
- Payment of past debts, at premium and compounded interest
- Transfer pricing, by which multinationals overprice their imports into the country and underprice exports
- Worsening balance of payments on account of worsening terms of trade
- Flight of capital because of speculation.

In other words, there are various ways in which externalised expenditure drains away the national income. Obviously then, there is little, or even negative, domestic saving.

A deeper, real-life analysis should lead to the conclusion that instead of looking for aid and foreign capital, it would be better from the national point of view to block, or reduce, some of the externalised expenditure, for example, blocking the use of the transfer price mechanism, or refusing to pay illegitimate foreign debts. Before seeking foreign aid or foreign private flows, it is necessary to address two questions:

1 Why is domestic expenditure so high? Is it because of war? Is it because the ruling elite, or a section of it, is very indulgent and wastes national income on unnecessary imports such as luxury cars and expensive consumables?
2   Why is there a high externalisation of funds? Is it justified? Is it because corrupt officials and/or private

sector operators are externalising funds? Is it because of repayment of interest on past debts that may have been incurred illegally or unjustifiably ('odious debt')? Is it because exporters are not bringing back into the country the full value of their exports? Is it because export earnings do not balance import expenditures?

Conclusion: What the facile tautological theory of 'the resource gap does is to provide a cover up for not digging deeper into the empirical reality, which is one of externalisation of resources and savings from Africa at a phenomenal rate, worse probably than even during the colonial days. This may be true of many other countries in the South.

Step 6 Creating institutions for investing national savings

Once all the leaky holes are plugged, it is also important to create in parallel institutions for ensuring that the national savings are properly invested. Investments are made by three principal actors or agencies:

- The state
- The private sector
- The community.

For the first, the state needs to raise revenue (mainly from taxes and tariffs). For the second, the private sector needs proper incentives and institutions to enable it to raise investment finance and facilities to invest it in ways that benefit private entrepreneurs as well the nation. Similarly, for community-based initiatives (rural as well as urban), there have to be incentives and facilities for gainful employment and generation of community wealth.

Orthodox economists focus on only the private sector to the exclusion of the other two. Why they do this is a question that needs to be asked. However, a small book like this cannot go into the political economy of 'the private sector as the engine of growth' ideology, which is formulated and disseminated by orthodox economists and global institutions such as the World Bank and the International Chamber of Commerce. So, instead of dwelling on private sector investments, this monograph focuses on the other two sectors that have been relatively neglected in the literature.

There is of course no denying that the private sector has a significant role to play, but in some situations – such as in Africa – an over-emphasis on the private sector leads to the dominance of the foreign private sector, and in particular of transnational corporations that have wealth, knowledge, and better political leverage than domestic private capital and local communities. This is why when many state assets in developing countries were privatised in the 1980s and 1990s as a result of pressure from the IMF and the World Bank, many of these assets (for example, in Zambia, Argentina, Korea and Thailand) were taken over by foreign private capitalists and bankers.

Looking back, some of these state assets should never have been privatised in the first place. Corruption, inefficiencies and incentives could have been handled differently. But that is water under the bridge; that is now history. What is necessary to state is that there has to be a balance between the state, private, and the community sectors. Indeed one of the important functions of the state is to nurture the growth of national capitalists. India had such a core group even before independence, but countries such as Taiwan-China, Korea and Malaysia went out of their way (through state subsidies and tariff protection) to create national champions who were then able not only to control the domestic market but also to capture a share in the export market.

In addition, the state should, among other things:

- Build a physical infrastructure of roads – including feeder roads that reach deep into the rural areas. The state should also provide the basic infrastructure system for public transport, basic equipment,

    telecommunications, and energy. This can generate
lower level manufacturing and service sector activities
in the private and community sectors.

- Develop a strong central bank which, together with
government ministries, can regulate the finance and
banking sector. The 1980s and 1990s idea that the central
bank should be independent of the state is a ludicrous
one. Once released from state control, the central banks
in many developing countries fell into the control of
the IMF. Indeed, in some African countries the IMF
placed its experts and advisers in their central banks to
monitor implementation of the structural adjustment
programmes, and control foreign exchange transactions.

- Build a network of social infrastructure in both the
rural and urban areas – schools, clinics, access to water
and energy for consumption and for industry and
agriculture, housing, community centres, consumer
protection, environmental protection, legal institutions,
etc.

- Build the nation's knowledge and research capacity,
especially in innovative research relevant to the skill sets
and resources available within their country and that is
independent of global knowledge producers such as the
World Bank and the OECD.

As for community investments, this is a much talked about subject but mainly in the context of the informal sector. This is unfor-
tunate, because it is not then taken seriously. The reality of life in
most developing countries is that it is this sector that fulfils the
basic needs of the bulk of the population – from the provision of
essential goods (such as kitchenware, agricultural tools) to services (such as transport, childcare, communication, etc). The state
in developing countries needs to upscale its support for communities by at least a hundred times. This is no exaggeration.

Step 7 Limiting aid to national democratic priorities

Having gone through the six steps, there remains the residual issue of whether there is any role that outside aid can play in ending aid dependence.

Before getting into that, it is important first to briefly discuss a theory propounded by some academics and institutions, namely that a heavy boost of foreign aid is the best way to get out of aid dependence. This is a variation of the 0.7 per cent theory. The quintessence of the booster theory is that it envisages a far greater flow of development aid for a concentrated period.

What is needed, the argument goes, is to fill the resource gap of, for example, Africa by a booster shot of foreign aid (calculated in billions of dollars) over a sustained period of say 10 to 15 years.[15] This money should be efficiently spent with minimal transaction costs and tightly controlled against abuse. (This is how the term 'aid efficiency' has entered the aid lexicography.) Under the collective supervision of the donors and the World Bank, and in partnership with the recipient countries, this money would then enable developing countries to put money where it was needed and where it would be efficiently used in line with the priorities of the recipient countries, who would own the process. The donors would collectively ensure the predictability of aid flows so that the recipient countries (it is mainly Africa that is the target) could undertake long term planning of the growth of their economies.

What would this achieve? It would, the argument goes, enable Africa to find its niche in the global market based on free competition, stable macroeconomic policies, and the creation of an enabling environment for private capital flows to come to Africa. Foreign private capital must, however, be provided with a reasonable return, which it must be able to repatriate, and guarantees over the safety of its investments against, for example, nationalisation. Private foreign capital must also be guaranteed the protection of its intellectual property rights. A combination of predictable official booster aid and the enterprise of the private sector (which would bring in FDIs and technology) would help

Africa build its supply side capacity, an infrastructure of roads, communications and port facilities ('trade facilitation' in the WTO jargon). It would also, with generous counselling and close monitoring by the developed countries, help Africa build, in the words of the 2008 World Bank Growth Report 'committed, credible, and capable governments'[16] based on the rule of law, democracy and openness to the market. These then are the basic ingredients that would finally enable Africa to discover its proper niche in the global market place, hopefully beyond the production and trade in raw materials. This 'aid' would then eventually extract Africa from aid dependence.

This, in essence, is the logic behind the OECD's Paris Declaration on Aid Effectiveness strategy, which we shall discuss later.

This, as is evident, is old medicine in new bottles marked 'efficiency', 'partnership', 'partner ownership', 'accountability', 'aid predictability', 'alignment', etc. However, this medicine contains two overdoses:

- An overdose in the quantity of aid, provided structures are first put in place for its efficient use and democratic governance as defined by the donors
- An overdose of donor monitoring, evaluation, and effective control.

Conclusion

In contrast to the donor strategy on development aid, the strategy proposed in this monograph puts the peoples of the developing countries in the driver's seat. This is a long haul: first, because it takes time and the evolution of independent political processes to empower people (the national project); and second, because the donors are not about to leave the driver's seat, which they have a vested interest in occupying.

To return to the question of whether, under this monograph's strategy, foreign aid would still have a role to play, I would say, yes it would, but in a radically different manner and modality.

The primary objective of the new style aid would be to empower the people (say of Africa) to realise their national project, defined broadly to include the region in which these nations are geographically located (for example, Eastern Africa in the case of Kenya, Uganda, Tanzania, Rwanda, Burundi and the Democratic Republic of Congo).

In this scenario, the following broad guidelines with respect to foreign aid would be consistent with the attainment of the national project. Going back to the rainbow colours, the position might be summarised as follows:

- **Red Aid (ideological aid)** should be completely proscribed as inadmissible. The nation (or the region) will decide the manner and pace of its integration into or out of the global market, including, if necessary, the use of tariff walls, subsidies, and protection for its industries. The nation (or the region) will also determine the pace and content of governance, including the shape and form of national and regional evolving democratic institutions without imperial interference.

- **Orange Aid** as a category should be abolished. It should simply be called by its proper name – commercial transactions. The spade should be called a spade. To take Africa as an example, this would apply whether these transactions are negotiated with traditional development partners, namely the OECD countries, or with the new ones, such as India, China and Brazil.

- **Yellow Aid (military and political)** that the nation decides (after democratic discussion right through to village level and through mass education) is necessary in order to liberate it from the imperial project.

- **Green/Blue Aid**, or the provision of GPGs and compensatory finance, may have an important role to play, provided progress is made at the international level to negotiate these and bring them under the control of new institutions of global governance. (This is further discussed in the last section of the book.) Thus, when grants, debt relief, humanitarian aid, emergency aid, aid for the welfare of refugees, aid for climate change, all come *not* tied to any procurement or ideological conditions, and when their content and use are fully determined by the recipient countries, these would all fulfil internationally agreed commitments for global public goods, and they would play an important role not only in the development of the developing countries but also in the promotion of global common good.

- **Purple Aid**, too, will have a major role to play, but strictly on the principle of solidarity. Its six categories have been discussed earlier. Here is where justice oriented foundations (many of them located in the US and Europe with their excellent philanthropic tradition) and civil society (or NGOs), both in the North and the South, can play a very positive role, particularly some of the large international NGOs, such as Oxfam, Action Aid, Christian Aid, Novib, etc. They can also play a role in educating the people, the parliaments and the media in developed countries about the realities on the ground and the need for the people in developing countries to find their own solutions from within the regions. But they must be a genuine solidarity movement. They must not become extended arms of their countries' foreign policies by tying their solidarity aid to human rights, and democratic governance conditionalities.[17]

Notes

1 Seven out of ten Filipinos believe that they are poor, according to the results of the latest IBON nationwide survey. The IBON January 2008 survey showed that 71.7 per cent of 1,503 respondents thought of themselves as poor, from 67.7 per cent in the January 2007 survey and 74.1 per cent

in October 2007. Moreover, 44.1 per cent of respondents said there were no available jobs or livelihood opportunities in their areas, 40.1 per cent said that there were livelihood opportunities or jobs but not enough, and only 12.3 per cent said that there were enough opportunities. See IBON (2008) 'People's political and economic perception (July and October 2007, and January 2008 Nationwide Survey)', http://info.ibon.org/images/survey/2007%20q4%20perception.pdf, accessed 17 July 2008.

2 UNDP (2003) *Human Development Report 2003 – Human Development Index*, 8 July, http://hdr.undp.org/en/media/hdr_2003_presskit_en.pdf.

3 Parthasarathy, S. (no date) 'National policies supporting smallholder dairy production and marketing: India case study', International Crops Research Institute for the Semi-Arid Tropics (ICRISAT), http://www.ilri.org/InfoServ/Webpub/Fulldocs/South_South/Ch25.htm, accessed 16 July 2008.

4 ILO (2007) 'Decent work for sustainable development, director-general's introduction to the International Labour Conference', 96th Session of the International Labour Conference, 30 May–15 June, (ILC 96-2007/Report I (A)), http://www.ilo.org/public/english/standards/relm/ilc/ilc96/pdf/rep-i-a.pdf, accessed 15 July 2008.

5 Daudey, E., and García-Peñalosa, C. (2005) 'The personal and the factor distributions of income in a cross section of countries', *The Journal of Development Studies*, vol. 43, no. 5.

6 ILO (2007).

7 Ibid.

8 Ibid.

9 'in ILO projects global economic turbulence could generate 5 million more unemployed in 2008', Web News from: ILO News in the world (2008) 24 January, http://un.by/en/ilo/news/world/11-01-08-new.html, accessed 15 July 2008.

10 See UNCTAD (2006) *Least Developed Country Report*, http://www.unctad.org/en/docs/ldc2006_en.pdf, accessed 15 July 2008.

11 Ibid.

12 Chang, Ha-Joon (2002) *Kicking Away the Ladder: Development Strategy in Historical Perspective*, London, Anthem.

13 Chang, Ha-Joon, (2005) *Why Developing Countries Need Tariffs: How NAMA negotiations could deny developing countries' right to a future*, Geneva, South Centre and Oxfam, p. xiii.

14 'For centuries, Africa has been integrated into the world economy mainly as a supplier of cheap labour and raw materials. Of necessity, this has meant the draining of Africa's resources rather than their use for the continent's development' (The New Partnership for Africa's Develoment (NEPAD) (2001) para 19, http://www.nepad.org/2005/files/documents/inbrief.pdf, accessed 15 July 2008). 'It is time that African resources are harnessed to create wealth for the well-being of her peoples' (para 20).

15 UNCTAD (2006) *Doubling Aid: Making the 'Big Push' Work*, New York and Geneva, United Nations.

16 World Bank (2008) *The Growth Report: Strategies for Sustained Growth and Inclusive Development*, p. 21.

17 Greenhill, R. (2005) *Real Aid: An Agenda for Making Aid Work*, Action Aid International UK.

CHAPTER 4

THE INTERNATIONAL AID ARCHITECTURE
Structures, processes and issues

The international aid architecture

As should be evident from the discussion so far, the matter of building the institutions of aid architecture arises primarily in relation to Green/Blue Aid.

Red (ideological) Aid has no claim to be considered as 'aid'. No country or group of countries has a right to impose its ideological perspective on other (usually weaker) states by means of aid, or through the instrumentality of agencies such as the IMF, the World Bank, the WIPO, and the OECD's Development Assistance Committee (DAC). Ideological imposition based on asymmetrical power and the threat of collateral sanctions is inherently unjust and illegitimate.

Orange (commercial) forms of transactions have no claim to be considered as aid. They are purely matters for bilateral, regional or multilateral negotiations between sovereign states, or between the private sector (corporations) and states, or among private sector corporations themselves.

Yellow (strategic and security-related) Aid may have some legitimate claim to be considered as aid under certain circumstances, and depending on the political perspectives of the parties to the negotiations.

Purple Aid, based on considerations of solidarity, has a highly legitimate claim to be considered as aid, but this is not some-

Table 3 Summary of the characteristics of different types of aid

Type of aid	Legitimacy of claim to be considered as development aid	Parties to the negotiations	Role for international organisations
Red (ideological) Aid	No legitimacy as aid	Between (unequal) sovereign states	No role for global IGOs (e.g. IMF, WB, WTO, WIPO, DCF, OECD)
Orange (commercial) Aid	No legitimacy as aid	Between commercial parties; also, state to state.	Only facilitative role (e.g. ITC, chamber of commerce)
Yellow (strategic/security) Aid	Depends on situation and political perspective	Between sovereign states	Role for political or military alliances
Green/Blue (GPGs, international legal commitments, compensatory finance) Aid	High degree of legitimacy as 'commitments'; but *not* as 'aid'	Intergovernmental negotiating machinery	Main function of IGOs within negotiated mandates
Purple (solidarity) Aid	High degree of legitimacy	State to state, people to people, people to state	No role for global IGOs

thing that is negotiated within the context of intergovernmental organisations. This is a matter between sovereign states, between people and people, and between people and states that are seeking allies in the struggle for justice and a voice in the international community.

An approximate tabulation of this is presented in Table 3. However, in the subsequent discussion, I shall examine the real world out there, not the ideal, preferred world that one would like to see. The challenge is how to move the architecture of international aid from the real to the ideal, from here to there. As with all matters of this kind, it is a struggle. And the struggle must begin here and now, with the recognition of the inequities of the real world.

Clearly, what is needed is a radical transformation not only of the prevailing notions and mind set about aid, but also the global architecture of aid. At present, development aid is not only decontextualised, distorted and monetised, but a labyrinthine edifice has been built around it to legitimise and operationalise it. Its success has been astounding. Thousands of people are engaged in the aid industry as defined by the dominant discourse, and thousands of papers written on a daily and monthly basis within the prevailing architecture and norms of the aid industry. There are also institutions where the good and the bad of foreign aid are intermingled. The aid industry churns out thousands of pages of literature including data, graphs, tables, econometric analysis, etc on a daily basis.[1] The dominant aid-dependent mindset and norms have given birth to an incredible number of false issues and false solutions.

An even more precarious part of this problematic paradigm is the institutionalisation of the architecture of the aid industry. Dominating this edifice is the World Bank, the IMF, and the OECD's DAC.

The World Bank

The World Bank Group is a family of five 'banks' that, as the bank's website says, provides finance and advice to countries for the purposes of economic development and eliminating poverty. The bank came into existence in December 1945 following the Bretton Woods agreements signed mainly between the developed countries. The term 'World Bank' generally refers to the International Bank for Reconstruction and Development (IBRD) and the International Development Association (IDA). The other banks are the International Finance Corporation (IFC), the Multilateral Investment Guarantee Agency (MIGA), and the International

Centre for Settlement of Investment Disputes (ICSID).

The World Bank's activities are focused on the developing countries, working, as the bank's website says, in fields such as human development (e.g. education and health), agriculture and rural development, environmental protection, infrastructure (e.g. roads, urban regeneration, electricity), and, significantly, governance (e.g. anti-corruption and development of legal institutions). Loans or grants for specific projects are usually linked to what are called conditionalities that tie aid to wider policy changes in the sector or the economy as a whole, or in governance structures. Also important to mention are the World Development Reports that the Bank produces annually on the economic condition of the world, and the World Bank Institute, the knowledge and ideological arm of the World Bank.

As we saw in an earlier section, it was the aid conditionalities of the IMF and the World Bank that stripped developing countries, especially in Africa, of tariff barriers and their other protective social and political-economic infrastructure even before the World Trade Organisation (WTO) stepped in to remove whatever defences they still had that might have saved their national economies from the ravages of globalisation. With their protective mechanisms destroyed, by the time we come to the escalating food and fuel prices of 2007–08, many developing countries were already too defenceless to protect themselves from these price surges.

It is also significant that over the last year the bank has made concessions on its voting formula without changing its highly skewed decision-making system in favour of the developed (or traditional donor) countries. It is also important to note that two countries – Venezuela and Ecuador – withdrew from the World Bank in April 2007.

The OECD-DAC

The OECD was created in 1948 to help administer the Marshall Plan for the reconstruction of Europe after the Second World War. It has evolved into a club of 23 rich countries that have endorsed the principles of representative democracy and a free market economy. The DAC is the principal coordinating body for OECD countries on issues related to cooperation with developing countries, including guidelines on best practices, collective learning and peer review mechanisms.

Despite its upfront economic profile, the OECD has several non-economic faces. For example, its Fragile States Group[2] is a forum that brings together experts on governance, conflict prevention and reconstruction in 'fragile states'. There is also the Network on Governance,[3] which covers issues such as taxation, accountability, human rights, development and the fight against corruption. The DAC publishes statistics and reports[4] on aid and other resource flows to developing countries and countries in transition.

What concerns us is the DAC Working Party on Aid Effectiveness (WPAE),[5] which was set up in 2003 following the Finance for Development consensus reached at Monterrey in December 2001. The WPAE is dominated by OECD donor countries and agencies, and the World Bank. However, it also has selected representatives from some recipient countries and civil society organisations (CSOs), all chosen by the DAC/World Bank duopoly. The WPAE oversees the implementation of the Paris Declaration on Aid Effectiveness (PDAE), adopted by DAC in March 2005, whose aim is to take 'far-reaching and monitorable actions to reform the ways we deliver and manage aid'.[6]

The Paris Declaration and the Accra Action Agenda

The OECD-DAC on its website gave three reasons why the Paris Declaration would make a difference in increasing the impact of aid. First, the PDAE went beyond a statement of general principles. It laid down a 'practical, action-orientated roadmap to improve the quality of aid and its impact on development'.[7] The 56 partnership commitments were clustered around five key principles: ownership, alignment, harmonisation, managing for results, and mutual accountability. Second, it set out 12 indicators to monitor progress in achieving results and 'encouraging progress against the broader set of partnership commitments'.[8] Third, it promised to create stronger mechanisms for accountability on the use of development resources. The PDAE recognised that the existing accountability requirements were often 'harder on recipients than donors'.[9] It also recognised that 'aid is more effective when partner countries exercise strong and effective leadership over their development policies and strategies'.[10]

On the face of it the Paris Declaration looked benign. It recognised the faults of the existing system, set out reasonably sensible principles on aid and, significantly, recognised the principle of ownership by the recipient countries, and of mutual accountability between donors and recipients. The PDAE formed the basis of the Accra Action Agenda (AAA), adopted as a 'consensus' document in September 2008. The Accra meeting was the biggest ever gathering of the aid industry, with almost 1,200 delegates from about 100 countries and UN agencies.

However, although the Triple A was defended as a 'moment of opportunity', a close analysis shows that the process was flawed and the South lost an opportunity to critically review the Paris Declaration from its development perspective. Indeed, in certain matters the AAA went beyond the PDAE in projecting the interests of the North.

Flawed process for the AAA

The AAA text was drafted by the WPAE outside the UN process, and outside the normal framework of international negotiations, such as over climate change, for example. Although references were made in the document to the United Nations and the Millennium Development Goals (MDGs), and the United Nations Development Programme had selectively participated in some of the processes, the PDAE/AAA was never part of the UN process. For example, many MDG-related objectives did not feature in the PDAE, especially MDG8, which deals with North–South relations where matters related to aid, trade and development are linked. In the AAA the North–South context was defined by the donors, which effectively meant the exclusion from the negotiating process of such important institutional groupings from the South as the Group of 77 and China. Many G77 countries were present in Accra, but only as individual countries. The developing countries were thus fragmented, whereas the developed countries generally presented a common front. The AAA contained a section on 'aid policies in fragile situations', but there was no representation in Accra of, for example, the African Union, which is a major stakeholder on this issue

Consequences of South disunity

For the developing countries to have turned the PDAE around to their benefit, three things had to have happened: first, the South governments needed to have acted together, for example through the Group of 77 and China; second, they needed to have worked closely with their CSOs (these chose, rather, to work through the OECD); and third, they needed to have subjected the PDAE to critical scrutiny and put aid in the larger context of development. None of these happened. The South's disunity had at least the following effects.

The AAA failed to locate aid in its larger developmental context. During the three days of the often closed-door official negotiations (like the World Trade Organisation's (WTO) 'green room' meetings) there was no serious discussion on what constituted development, why aid was still necessary after five decades of its failure to deliver development, and how countries might get out of aid dependence as opposed to just making it more 'effective'. The implication was that aid had become a permanent feature of North–South relations. There was much talk about the need for aid to address issues of poverty and the MDGs, but there was no discussion on, for example, the link between aid, debt, trade and poverty and North–South relations.

Even as the AAA was being negotiated in Accra, the WTO trade negotiations on the Doha round in Geneva had collapsed. Two significant issues accounted for this. One was the so-called 'special products' – products that are sensitive to the survival of millions of smallholder farmers in developing countries. The rich countries had demanded that for their agricultural and industrial products to have access to the markets of the poor countries, the latter must limit how many products they might classify as 'special'. The poor countries (organised around the Group of 33 – G33) had resisted this. It would have meant lowering tariffs further for non-special products, which would have intensified the further destruction of their industries and agriculture. The other contentious issue related to cotton. The US domestic subsidy for cotton for a few hundred of its farmers had depressed cotton prices in the global market, depriving millions of African (among other) farmers of fair prices for their exports and sinking them into poverty. The negotiations collapsed in July 2008, precisely on the issues of 'special products' and cotton, and yet in Accra, only a few weeks later, the delegates behaved as if aid and trade existed in two separate compartments and had no causal connection with poverty.

There was no discussion in Accra about the ideological content of aid. There was much talk about 'untying aid', but this was limited to unlinking aid from the procurement of goods and services paid out of aid. There was no discussion of untying aid from its ideological content, from Red Aid. Accra failed to acknowledge that over the last 20–25 years, neoliberal globalisation had deindustrialised and de-agriculturised the most trade-vulnerable countries of the world, and that aid was part of it. The argument that the best way for poor countries to enter the global value chain on a competitive basis is through free trade is a self-serving ideology of those who control institutions of economic governance – the IMF, the World Bank, the OECD and the WTO – and their intellectual ideologues in universities and think tanks. Aid is one of the instruments for enforcing this ideology on the countries of the South.

The AAA recognised that 'additional work' was required 'to improve the methodology and indicators of progress of aid effectiveness'. However, the South failed to take up the challenge. The following are among the PDAE/AAA's most serious flaws.

1 The performance conditionalities are prepared by the donors and the World Bank. The compliance tests on public financial management, budget execution procedures, audit monitoring and evaluation, procurement and social and environmental assess-ment are based on 12 criteria or indicators and a rating system developed by the DAC/World Bank and not on the economic and social policies of the recipient countries. In one African case, for example, there is a 12-page matrix, plus 49 pages on accounting on good progress. Failing these criteria, the recipient countries are subject to penalties, including the withdrawal of aid. In con-trast, there are no penalties for donor defaults. In other words, contrary to PDAE's stated principle, there was no real mutual accountability.

2 The PDAE opened the back door to issues rejected by the developing countries in the WTO. For example, the devel-oping countries had rejected the so-called Singapore issues of investment policy, competition policy and government procurement. There are also contested provisions in the WTO's Trade Related Intellectual Property Rights agreement, especially concerning intellectual property enforcement. The PDAE/AAA provided an alternative route for these contested areas to be smuggled into recipient countries through the aid channel.

3 No effort was made in Accra to discuss the implications of a shift from project lending to direct budget support. There are three inter-related issues here: a pooling of donor resources; an injection of this pool into the national budget, which oblig-es the recipient countries to discuss their strategies with the donors and the World Bank; and the provision for scaling up activities and funding, based on collective donor assessment of good or bad policies. Nobody drew attention to the danger

that if the performance of the recipients fell short of targets on, for example, health matters or the MDGs, then direct budget support could become the instrument for stopping aid. Already, the World Bank's Comprehensive Development Strategies and Aid Effectiveness Reviews showed that in the poverty reduction strategies assessment undertaken by it, '... few of them provide the level of operational detail that specifies how objectives are to be achieved through policy actions'.[11] Growth performance was apparently lower than donor expectations. The implication is that if this were still the case by 2010, the donors would demand better performance or stop aid.

4 Aid predictability was the new mantra of PDAE/AAA, but what did this mean in practice? At first sight it looked like a progressive step because, as the argument went, it would enable the recipient partner countries to undertake medium to long-term planning. However, the prospect of the minister of finance and a team of officials in a poor African country sitting across from a DAC team consisting of experts representing 23 of the wealthiest countries in the world and the World Bank is a scenario of classical power asymmetry. A small country is hardly in a position to negotiate with the phalanx of wealthy donors. If the national development budget is strained, the promise of 'predictable' aid is a temptation hard to resist. Second, the AAA had put no system in place to ensure that the 'predicted' aid would actually materialise. What if a change of government in an OECD country led to a review of its commitment or to a tying of its direct budget support to certain conditions, say on immigration or environment? What is the small recipient country then supposed to do? Third, as long as aid continued to remain an instrument for persuading the partner country to conform to governance, human rights, protection of intellectual property rights, and other Northern values

(Red Aid), is not the partner country creating conditions for its own recolonisation?

5 The AAA added some of its own original language to the PDAE. Paradoxically, instead of weakening the power of the donors it reinforced it. The following are the more important examples.

First, there was much discussion in Accra on whether to use recipient country systems for aid-financed procurement. In a compromise text it was agreed to use country systems 'to the maximum extent possible'. This provided a convenient escape option to donors. The Millennium Challenge Account, for example, is tied to US procurement procedures, and German technical assistance is compulsorily channelled through GTZ. The 'maximum extent possible' wording allows them to argue that they are 'trying their maximum' and are AAA-compatible. As in the WTO, the AAA has no means to enforce or verify 'best endeavour' clauses.

Second, the AAA brought through the back door the controversial issue of financing for climate change and, in effect, might have undermined the position of the G77 and China that financing for climate change must come through UN channels, such as the UNFCCC. Against this the North and the World Bank set up their own funds, outside the UN, over which they have control. The developing countries finance ministers who were in Accra were probably not fully briefed on the full implications of the following statement in the AAA: 'As new global challenges emerge, donors will ensure that existing channels for aid delivery are used and, if necessary, strengthened before creating separate new channels that risk further fragmentation and complicate co-ordination at country level.' The implications are clear for those familiar with the negotiations on climate change: that financing for technology transfer for climate change would remain voluntary and aid-based; that finances would be channelled through the World Bank, giving it a new lease of life; and that these would come with the usual World Bank conditionalities.

Third, the AAA recognised the significance of South–South cooperation but did not extend its principles to North–South relations. The AAA noted that South–South cooperation was based on the principles of non-interference in internal affairs, equality, national sovereignty, cultural diversity and identity. However, it did not say if these principles also applied to North–South cooperation, only that South–South cooperation was 'a valuable complement to North–South cooperation'. In effect, then, the AAA endorsed the idea that North–South cooperation was based on different principles, including intervention in the internal affairs of the recipient countries, especially on matters related to human rights, rule of law and democracy (Red Aid).

Fourth, perhaps the most audacious section of the AAA was the one related to 'aid policies for countries in fragile situations'. Without the slightest hint that it might smack of an imperialist project, the AAA stated that 'Donors will provide demand-driven, tailored and co-ordinated capacity-development support for core state functions and for early and sustained recovery. They will work with developing countries to design interim measures that are appropriately sequenced and that lead to sustainable local institutions.' Whilst the challenge of nation building is recognised (see pp. 66–75), it is too important and sensitive a matter to leave to the donors as part of their aid strategy. The failed efforts at 'state-building' of the US-led 'alliance of the willing' in Afghanistan, Iraq, Somalia and other countries should have warned the developing countries against an endorsement of such a blatant declaration of the use of aid to build North-designed core state functions in the South.

The role of civil society at Accra

As indicated earlier, the CSOs, even those from the South, came to Accra via the OECD-appointed advisory group. The CSOs that were consulted by WPAE before Accra had made five critical, and important, points about the Paris Declaration,[12] among them that it lacked vision, democratic ownership, transparency and ambition on conditionality and the untying of aid. At the Accra meeting, however, the CSOs were largely irrelevant to the official process and the government-negotiated outcome. One Canadian NGO that was part of the advisory group described the overall CSO reaction to the AAA as 'very disappointing.'[13] Did the NGOs really believe they would change the character of the PDAE/ AAA? Past experience with World Bank and donor-driven processes, such as the PRSP (see p. 81), should have taught them that these processes end up in co-opting them in legitimising a predetermined donor agenda. History, alas, is a poor teacher. Against faith and hope, experience is a weak competitor.

The Development Cooperation Forum (DCF)

The DCF was created at the October 2005 World Summit as a forum of the United Nations Economic and Social Council (ECOSOC) to review trends in international development cooperation, including strategies, policies and financing, promote greater coherence among the development activities of different development partners and strengthen the normative and operational link in the work of the United Nations.[14] The DCF was mandated to provide policy guidance and options as well as recommendations on practical measures to enhance the coherence and effectiveness of international development cooperation. It was further asked to see how the internationally agreed development goals (IADGs), including the MDGs, might be realised. Furthermore, it was asked to provide a platform for member states to exchange lessons learned and share experiences in formulating, supporting and implementing national development strategies

Located within the Department of Economic and Social Affairs, the DCF has an advisory board of people from various stakeholders including governments, intergovernmental organisations and NGOs to advise the secretary-general. (I have been on the advisory board since its inception.)

The DCF will be considered more closely in the discussion on reform of the aid architecture.

Restructuring the architecture: parallelism and reform

For the last 60 years the world has lived under an aid architecture crafted in the years immediately following the Second World War. It started with the creation of the OECD in 1948, to help administer the Marshall Plan for the reconstruction of Europe, and the Bretton Woods institutions. Of the latter, the IMF was to provide international liquidity in times of crisis and exogenous shocks, and World Bank development capital. These antiquated structures have lost much of their legitimacy and relevance. There are two principal reasons for this.

First, it is now evident that the 60-year-old development architecture has failed. Under the present phase of globalisation (c. 1985–2005), and despite claims made by the principal dispensers of development aid (OECD and the World Bank Group), the disparity between and within nations has increased. Development has continued to elude most developing countries, especially the weak and vulnerable, which do not have a say in the decision-making processes of these institutions.

The remarkable, and indeed tragic, aspect of the continuing poverty of more than a third of humanity is that there is no rational or sane cause for this. Never in the annals of human history has science and technology developed at such pace. It has evolved in quantum leaps. And yet whilst we have automated production in agriculture in one part of the world, in another, vast numbers of poor peasants use hoes for cultivation and bullock-cart traction that go back millennia. Given advances in science and their application to food production, healthcare and medical research, education, energy, housing, town planning, etc there is no reason why millions should perish for want of food, medicine and shelter or from natural calamities. In the meantime, the top 50 financial institutions control almost $50 trillion in assets, roughly a third of global total, and the world's 1,100 richest individuals own almost twice the assets of the poorest 2.5 billion, a morally offensive by-product of the leave-it-to-the-market ideology of these institutions.

The second reason is that, in spite of all the obstacles and challenges that the developing countries have faced over the last 60 years, some of them have been able to end their aid dependence. They are now the new players with capital funds to make an impact on the inflows and outflows of capital. Eighty per cent of the world's dollar reserves, for example, are now held not by G7 central banks but by emerging economies. However, they are not represented in the OECD, and have no real clout in the IMF and the World Bank. The belated attempt in 2008 to make a marginal change in the voting system in the IMF is a travesty of equity. These emerging countries of India, China, Brazil and Russia may have to create parallel institutions to the World Bank.

The OECD

In the long run, the OECD-DAC's function, or at least its leading role in international aid and development cooperation issues, will wither away. As long as the DAC continues to sit in the driver's seat on the matter of development cooperation, it will be perceived to be an instrument of the imperial project. The intellectual and political leaders of the OECD not only realise this but also acknowledge it as something that has to change. It is for this reason that they give so much significance to the concept of ownership of the development agenda by what it now prefers to call its 'partners'. They have rightly concluded that ownership has to pass from the donors to the partners.

This admission, however, puts the OECD in a dilemma. If the ownership of development aid does pass completely into the hands of the partners, including coordination, monitoring, and evaluation, then the DAC will be out of business. It will have made itself redundant. It could, perhaps, play a subsidiary role in structures that the recipient countries might create to coordinate aid, but playing second fiddle would not sit well with DAC members' sense of self respect, or with their domestic populations. In any case, the DAC would no longer be what it is today. It will slowly be put out of business as an aid coordinating agency, and become a policy coordinating body solely for its member states.

If, on the other hand, the DAC is reluctant to leave the driver's seat on aid issues, then it must create the *appearance* of passing over ownership to the partners whilst keeping all powers of decision making, monitoring and evaluation tightly in its control. If appearances or illusions can serve the same purpose as reality, then why transfer effective power over to the partners? This is where the idea of the Paris Declaration on Aid Effectiveness had its genesis.

However, the OECD's hegemony in the development aid architecture may not endure for long. The PDAE strategy is too closely linked with the discredited institutions of the World Bank and the IMF. It creates potential for conflict either with its partner countries or with the new players (Brazil, Russia, India and China – BRIC) especially over the OECD-World Bank Red Aid conditionalities. Red Aid, or aid with ideological conditions, we argued earlier is like the poisoned chalice of the aid industry and mainly responsible for widening inequities between and within nations. Also, it comes loaded with such sensitive matters as human rights, Western-style democracy and the rule of law as defined by Western norms. The BRIC countries are unlikely to play the Western game of holding the partners to account on such matters, as the examples of the Sudan and Zimbabwe illustrate.

In fact what the OECD countries expected is quite extraordinary and completely impractical. They wanted the BRIC countries not only to join them in disciplining errant smaller to middle-sized states in the South (including failed and dictatorial states, especially in Africa), but also argue that China and Russia too should allow their human rights record and their rule of law to be subjected to scrutiny by them. This from the beginning was an unlikely scenario.

In the end, the traditional donors of the OECD might have to settle for a second best option, namely, closing their eyes to human rights violations and dictatorships in developing countries, leaving these delicate and sensitive matters to the local populations and the internal democratic processes and/or the regional political leadership. Sooner or later the OECD governments will come under pressure from their business corporations that matters of human rights, etc are irrelevant to business, and that they cannot afford to lose business in conditions of increasing competition for resources and markets, especially in Africa. The example of the British company Anglo-American Corporation making a $40 million investment in the mining industry in Zimbabwe in June 2008 at the very time that the British government was contemplating further sanctions against the government of President Mugabe illustrates this emerging tension between governments and corporations in the OECD countries.

Paradoxically, this second option (closing OECD eyes to abuses of human rights, etc) would not necessarily be a negative development. Although this would profoundly disappoint civil society organisations in the West, they should understand that to try to be the custodians of good behaviour on the part of governments in the South, as judged by a Western yardstick, is bound to perpetuate the image of Europe and the US as imperialist countries. The people of the developing countries must be left to create their own institutions of just government.

In practice, the OECD countries have very little choice in the matter. They might try and use the PDAE and the AAA and their hidden sanctions (for example, the threat of withholding budget support) in order to reproduce their conception of good government, but this is likely to backfire. In the cases of, say, present-day Sudan or Zimbabwe, they had to plead with neighbouring countries to intervene amidst growing frustration with their own inability to influence the situation. They cannot (as they could during the heyday of the empire) simply drop paratroopers to discipline errant behaviour by rebels and dictators in the Third World, unless they have support from some or all countries in the region (as the US intervention in Somalia with the aid of other African states illustrates).

The World Bank

If the OECD is in trouble as an aid-related agency, the World Bank faces an even bleaker future. Above all, it depends for its funds from either member government contributions, or from borrowing on the open market. Furthermore, its ideological position that trade and capital liberalisation is good for the developing countries is fast losing intellectual support. For example, Dani Rodrik of Harvard University and Arvind Subramanian of the Peterson Institute published an appraisal of financial globalisation.[15] They concluded that it is far from obvious that developing countries benefit much from opening up to global capital. Many countries in the South prefer to either borrow directly from the market or from each other rather than from the World Bank with all its conditionalities.

A lifeline that could save the World Bank is the new role it hopes it can play on funding climate change. How the global governance structure on climate change will shape up is still a hot issue, especially since the 2007 Bali conference. One of the most contentious issues is how to finance the huge costs involved in moving to a new, low-carbon global economy – mitigation, adaptation, risk management and risk insurance; technology development, deployment, diffusion and transfer; and capacity building. We are looking at trillions not billions of dollars of potential business for those that would be involved in climate change financing.[16]

The World Bank, supported by most of the OECD donor community, is hoping to harness this opportunity to stimulate its otherwise gloomy future. On the other hand, the developing countries (and this monograph) are arguing that the provision of new, additional, adequate and predictable financing by the developed countries that are parties to the UN Framework Convention on Climate Change (UNFCCC) is a legally binding commitment under Art. 4.7 of the Convention, and that global funding for climate change should be placed in the UNFCCC framework and not in the World Bank.

The IMF

The IMF is also in the midst of a dual crisis. First, its credibility is at its lowest point, and second, most developing countries do not need it any more. What has destroyed the IMF's credibility is venturing beyond its original mandate – 'mission creep' – which the US Congressional Meltzer Commission had spotted as the IMF's major weakness (see p. 62). The commission noted that the IMF had 'little expertise' as a development institution.

Nonetheless, until there is an alternative system at the global level that can provide liquidity at times of crisis and exogenous shocks, the IMF might still have a role to play, provided it pulled back to its original mandate. Although some alternative arrangements are beginning to appear, especially at the regional level, such as the Banco del Sur created at the initiative of Venezuela and joined by several key regional players under the Mercosur framework, these initiatives are still in their early stages and need to be tested over time.[17]

A truth commission should be established to evaluate the work of the IMF over the last 50 years, including the impact of its policies and prescriptions on the development of the countries of the south. The truth commission should have the power to solicit information and hear witnesses, to investigate, publicise, and refer to the abuses in the use of international funds and the powers of the international financial institutions. The IMF should wind down and terminate all the programmes and activities it has created in its 'mission creep' since 1971. These include its Structural Adjustment Facility; Enhanced Structural Adjustment Facility; Structural Adjustment Programmes; Poverty Reduction Strategy Papers; the imposition of so-called good governance policies; loans for purposes other than the IMF's original mandate of addressing short-term external trade imbalances; bail-outs of banks and private lenders; and advice, prescriptions, and mandates on national economic policies.

The IMF should be redesigned not as a centralising but as a coordinating institution. In order words, practically all of the present functions of the IMF that can move out of Washington should be regionalised at the continental level. This process can begin first, for example, in Latin America and Asia, with elements of an African initiative put in place by the African Union for the African continent. These should create their own regional credit institutions and buffer reserves to protect against exogenous shocks, some of them emanating from the precariousness of speculative finance in the present global system.

The IMF's primary function would then be coordinating of the functions of the regional financial bodies. The debate would then shift from reforming the voting formula of the IMF (a futile exercise in any case) to how the IMF would coordinate with regional financial institutions in the management of the global reserve funds to protect national and regional economies from exogenous shocks and financial volatility.

The Development Cooperation Forum (DCF)

At the time of writing there was no institution at international level that had the credibility or legitimacy to discuss, plan, give advice or coordinate development cooperation. One body with the potential to play that role was the DCF. However, it faced many challenges:

- As a relatively new institution it could not afford to load itself with onerous responsibilities.
- It had a very small secretariat and very little resources, of which most came from traditional donors.
- It had to function within the UN framework, which gave it legitimacy on the one hand, but also exposed it to the risk of becoming a football between contending forces of the 'West and the Rest' – the G7 countries of the North and the G77 countries of the South.

Nonetheless, the DCF had to take up the challenge and offer its facilities for these contending forces to find a middle ground in the short run. In the long run, and if the G77 countries took it seriously, the DCF could take over as an alternative to the OECD-DAC World Bank duopoly in the aid architecture. Like the DAC of the OECD, the DCF should not provide an aid coordinating mechanism (because that would be impractical if not impossible). It should, rather, focus on providing *conceptual clarity* on issues related to development.

It has been suggested by the South Centre in a study undertaken in 2007[18] that the DCF should link aid with broader issues of finance for development, and put aid into perspective (e.g. in relation to the mobilisation of domestic resources, trade, investments, diaspora remittances, brain drain, and the larger systemic issues of financial architecture). In relation to the issue of 'development aid' specifically, the study recommended that:

- The DCF needs to question the conceptual and operational aspects of DAC's definitions of aid and development.
- It should distance itself from the PDAE.
- It should facilitate debate and discourse on the governance aspects of international development cooperation, which at present is largely donor driven.
- It must address the question of national democratic ownership of the development process.
- It must address the domination of the value systems of the North and the three kinds of asymmetries – power asymmetry,[19] economic asymmetry and knowledge asymmetry – in relation to development cooperation.

The South Centre also suggested that the DCF should encourage an independent study of its own on how the developing countries can end aid dependence.

In a report by the secretary-general on the DCF,[20] the following quotations from the sobering analysis of the PDAE point in the right direction.

- 'Paris Declaration negotiations did not engage all stakeholders.'
- 'The aid effectiveness agenda has yet to change donor behaviour.'
- 'The tying of large portions of aid is unreported.'
- 'Policy conditionality is a key cause of unpredictability. Conditions associated with governance indicators have proliferated.'
- 'There is no current agreement on what constitutes concessional lending.'
- 'Cross-cutting development issues are not sufficiently reflected in the current aid effectiveness framework.'
- 'Aid coordination is increasingly led by programme countries, yet negotiation capacities remain limited. Capacity-building tends to focus on the central government. Many development goals are incidental to strategies and policies.'
- 'Poverty reduction strategy papers fail to focus on the broader development goals.'
- 'Donor policies also fail to focus on the internationally agreed development goals.'
- 'Performance assessments focus primarily on processes, institutions and policies.'

Here is a good beginning for the future of the DCF, but it is no more than an opening preamble to what will be a long drawn process of correcting knowledge, economic and power asymmetries that exist between the developing and the developed countries.

South–South cooperation

This is a growing area with huge potential, especially since the existing institutions of global economic governance are losing both credibility and effectiveness as agencies to promote equitable development. The report mentioned above by the UN secretary general on development cooperation highlighted the following as some of the salient features of South–South cooperation:

- Concessional lending for South–South development cooperation carries less risk of making debt unsustainable
- South–South development cooperation balances flexibility and predictability
- Absence of policy conditionality in South–South cooperation, although procurement is mostly tied to contributing countries' goods and services.

The secretary general's paper, however, is trapped in the OECD-DAC's vocabulary and flawed definition of development cooperation. It is therefore not able to capture the full essence of South–South cooperation. For example, following DAC's definition, it left out assistance that is based on the principle of solidarity (Purple Aid), and political-military aid (Yellow Aid) to support countries of the South that are still struggling to free themselves from the imperial project. This is not factored into the UN's calculations. Also, the UN did not take into account the provision of concessional credit by certain countries in Latin America, to countries in the region and in the Caribbean, to purchase oil during the 2007–2008 period of rising fuel prices. Similarly, the support provided by, for example, Brazil, China, India and South Africa, and other developing countries to one another, in the form of financial and technology transfers that are based on solidarity, and not purely commercial interests, need to be factored into the equation. These are very important aspects of South–South cooperation. Here the quantity of aid is not as significant as its political importance.

In other words, the United Nations too, has to get out of its conceptual dependence on categories, definitions and methodologies of collecting data developed by the donors (OECD), and the World Bank.

Notes

1 Roger Riddell says he read 20,000 pages on the subject whilst writing his book. Riddell, R. (2007) *Does Foreign Aid Really Work?*, Oxford, Oxford University Press, p. xviii.

2 See http://www.oecd.org/dac/fragilestates.

3 See http://www.oecd.org/dac/governance.

4 See http://www.oecd.org/dac/stats.

5 See http://www.oecd.org/dac/effectiveness.

6 OECD (2005)'Paris Declaration on Aid Effectiveness – ownership, harmonisation, alignment, result and mutual accountability', http://www.oecd.org/dataoecd/0/27/34504737.pdf, accessed 16 July 2008.

7 (2007) 'Development effectiveness in practice – applying the Paris Declaration to advancing gender equality, environmental sustainability and human rights', para 2, concept note for the Dublin workshop, 26-27 April, http://www.oecd.org/dataoecd/42/16/38408110.pdf, accessed 16 July 2008.

8 OECD-DAC (no date) 'Three reasons why the Paris Declaration will make a difference significantly increasing the impact of aid', http://www.oecd.org/document/18/0,3343,fr_2649_3236398_35401554_1_1_1_1,00.html, accessed 16 July 2008.

9 Ibid.

10 Ibid.

11 Pambazuka News (2008)'The Paris Declaration and aid effectiveness', 10 June, http://www.pambazuka.org/en/category/features/48634, accessed 16 July 2008.

12 Advisory Group on Civil Society and Aid Effectiveness (2007) 'Civil society and aid effectiveness; concept paper', http://web.acdi-cida.gc.ca/cs.

13 Morton, Bill (2008) 'The Accra HLF: good news for aid effectiveness, or a victory for mediocrity?', North-South Institute, http://northsouthinstitute.wordpress.com/2008/09/10/the-accra-hlf-good-news-for-aid-effectiveness-or-a-victory-for-mediocrity/, accessed 1 October 2008.

14 General Assembly Resolution A/Res/60/1 of October 2005, and General Assembly Resolution A/Res/61/16 of January 2007.

15 Rodrik, Dani and Subramanian, Arvind (2008) 'Why did financial globalization disappoint?', *Development Industry*, http://ksghome.harvard.edu/~drodrik/Why_Did_FG_Disappoint_March_24_2008.pdf.

16 South Centre (2008) 'Financing the global climate change response: suggestions for a Climate Change Fund (CCF)', South Centre Analytical Note.

17 Girvan, Norman (2008) 'Alba, Petrocaribe, and Caricom: issues in a new dynamic', *South Centre Bulletin*, 16 June.

18 South Centre (2007) 'Reshaping the international development cooperation architecture: perspectives on a strategic development role for the Development Cooperation Forum (DCF)'; and South Centre (2008) 'Perspectives on the role of the Development Cooperation Forum: building strategic approaches to enhancing multilateral development cooperation'.

19 Girvan, Norman (2006) 'Power Imbalances and Development Knowledge', Canada, North-South Institute. Professor Girvan provides a conceptual framework for the analysis of power imbalance in the international development architecture and summarises Southern reviews on its reform.

20 UN Department of Economic and Social Affairs (2008) 'Trends and progress in international development cooperation, E/2008/69.

CHAPTER 5

SUMMARY AND CONCLUSIONS
The future of aid

This chapter summarises the main analysis and conclusions we draw from our study. The study is aimed at provoking a serious rethinking of the whole issue of development aid.

1 For far too long the debate on development aid has been constrained by conceptual traps and the limitations of the definitions provided by the donors. If the recipients or beneficiaries of aid are to own the process, as present trends in the development literature suggest, then the conceptual reframing of the issues must itself change its location from the North to the South. This study is a start.

2 The conceptual starting point is not aid but development. The horse of development must be put before the cart of aid. Growth, admittedly, is an important aspect of development, and indeed there is no need to labour the point (as some orthodox economists and the World Bank attempt to do defensively). But growth is not the same as development. In this study, we have defined development, following in the footsteps of Julius Nyerere, the founding president of Tanzania and the first chairman of the South Centre, as 'a long democratic process, that starts "from within", where people participate in the decisions that affect their lives, without imperial interference from outside, and aimed at improving the lives of the people and realisation of the potential for self support, free from fear of want and political, economic and social exploitation'.

We put it as a formula: Development = SF + DF − IF, where SF is the social factor − the essential well-being of the people; DF is the democratic factor – the right of the people to participate in decision-making that affects their lives; and IF is the imperial factor – the right of nations to self-determination and liberation from imperial domination.

This is in sharp contrast to the mainstream orthodox economists' definition as Development = Growth + Wealth accumulation, where Growth = Open markets + Foreign investments + Good governance (as defined by the West), and the wealth accumulation by the rich is assumed to 'filter through' to the poor by market-driven forces.

3 The most critical aspect of our definition of development is its political economy and historical context. The developing countries have gained their political independence, but in most cases they are still trapped in an asymmetrical economic, power and knowledge relationship with the former colonial powers that continue to dominate the process of globalisation, and the institutions of global governance (the IMF, the World Bank, the WTO, WIPO, WCO, OECD, EU Commission, etc). The developing countries are making heroic efforts to disengage from this lock-in situation (demanding policy space, for example). Some of them (the so-called newly emerging industrialised countries of the South) have indeed succeeded or partly succeeded, but the bulk of the developing countries are still trapped in the shackles of history. Africa, especially, is identified as a continent that has not fared well.

From this trap, Africa and others can liberate themselves only if they take matters of development into their own hands – and do not leave it to aid and its delimiting and colonising conditionalities, such as the structural adjustment programmes of the IMF and the World Bank, and the Paris Declaration on Aid Effectiveness as also endorsed by the Accra Action Agenda.

4 In other words, the national project, the project for self-determination, is still on the agenda of political action for developing countries. Its counter, the imperial project, is also still alive, but gradually weakening. Its ideology – the Washington consensus

and globalisation – crafted after the dominant paradigm of free market liberalism and Western systems of governance, democracy and the rule of law, has lost credibility and legitimacy. This is not to undervalue the importance of democracy or the rule of law. Without these there would be anarchy and oppression. But these values cannot be imposed on the developing countries from outside, and certainly not loaded on to the wagon called 'development aid', followed by sanctions against those who fall short of Western donor expectations. The experience of Zimbabwe, tragic in its consequences, is an example of the curse of Red Aid, swallowed by a government and a people who had sacrificed so much to win their political independence. It is for this reason that the case of Zimbabwe has been analysed in detail in this monograph.

5 The fundamental reason why the relationship between 'aid' and 'development' is not fully understood is because of the way both terms are defined in the OECD-DAC vocabulary, definitions which have also been adopted by the United Nations. These are self-serving, West-centric, value-loaded and arbitrary definitions. It is argued here, for example, that there is no good reason for excluding what I call Yellow Aid (or military and political aid) from the definition. This kind of arbitrary exclusion ignores the military and political assistance provided by countries in the South to, for example, the liberation of Southern Africa. Worse still, it places military aid under the carpet, outside of a rational discourse within its political and ethical context.

6 In this context, it is argued that the 0.7 per cent has acquired a 'mythical' status. It carries an ethical-moral dimension, and provokes a lot of passion, particularly among civil society and in the North. This is an understandable reaction from NGOs and civil society organisations that have a strong affinity with the South on grounds of solidarity, but they have an imperfect understanding of the structural problems with the aid architecture. For the developing countries, the 0.7 per cent is a weapon to hold the North to their promises, even when the last 40 years' experience should

have made them wiser. An extended and expanded version of the 0.7 per cent model is the 'booster' model of aid. This is based on the assumption that the 'resource gap' in developing countries (in particular, Africa) should be filled by a massive dose of aid over a number of years until the countries take off, like an aeroplane. The proponents of both the 0.7 per cent and the booster models need to question the 'resource gap' theory. They will then understand that the developing countries do not have a resource gap. It is a gap unwittingly or deliberately created, directly as a result of the activities of global corporations and the misdirected policies of the IMF and World Bank. The irony is that the booster aid is still packaged within the framework of the very conditionalities that are part of the problem and not the solution.

7 This monograph provides a new taxonomy for development aid – in five hues – in a more rational and comprehensive classification. Development aid is placed along a continuum from Purple Aid (based on solidarity) on the extreme left and Red Aid (ideological aid) on the extreme right. In between are Orange Aid (which is really not aid at all, and should simply be called commercial transactions); Yellow Aid (already explained above); and Green/Blue Aid (whose three components – the provision of global public goods, non-tied humanitarian and emergency aid, and compensatory finance – are segments of the totality of financial and technical and technological assistance that are genuinely developmental. These are part of the global good not only from the national (recipient) country's perspective, but also from the global perspective. One implication of this classification, for example, is that global civil society in the North as well in the South might find they have more affinity with Purple Aid, and perhaps also with Green/Blue Aid, than with aid of the other three colours.

8 The body of the book consists of the seven steps that the developing countries need to take in order to exit aid dependence. The most difficult is the first step – the psychology of aid dependence.

The dependence psychology has not only occupied the minds of leaders in many (if not most) developing countries, but it has also taken roots in mass psychology. It is not necessary to attempt to summarise the seven steps. Much more can be written on the subject than is contained in this monograph. The important point is that the process has to begin somewhere. It is an agenda that has to be captured by the people themselves at community and grassroots level. However, it also requires an enlightened and visionary leadership at national, regional, and continental levels.

9 It is argued here that the present aid and development architecture at the international level is an obstacle to the realisation of the national project. Three power asymmetries – economic power, political power and knowledge power – are deeply embedded in the existing structures. It is a continuing battle for the developing countries to try and secure policy space within the constraints imposed by these asymmetrical structures.

10 The debate on the Paris Declaration on Aid Effectiveness (PDAE) is located in this larger context to explain the circumstance in which the OECD's Development Assistance Committee (DAC) and the World Bank and IMF have been trying to retain their relevancy and legitimacy, both of which were severely eroded in the 1980s as a result of the changing geopolitical and economic realities, and the failure of their development strategies in the South. For the DAC its oblivion is a historical necessity, in any event. At best, it might remain as a body to coordinate policies for OECD member countries. As for the World Bank and the IMF, they might salvage themselves if they pull out of Red Aid, withdraw to their original missions, and give voice to those who have suffered most from the developmental failure of their policies and the financial volatility of the last two decades of the 20th century and the first decade of the 21st.

11 In this broad historical and political perspective, the Development Cooperation Forum (DCF) of the UN and the fast evolving South–South relationship can play a very positive role. However, the DCF faces many challenges, and its future is still largely uncertain.

12 At the end of the day, we need a truly heterogeneous, pluralistic global society that is based on the shared values of our civilisation, and the shared fruits of the historical development of the productive forces of science, technology and human ingenuity. Only on this basis can we build a global society that is free from want, exploitation, insecurity and injustice.

SOUTH CENTRE

The South Centre is an intergovernmental organisation of developing countries established in 1995 with its headquarters in Geneva. It has grown out of the work and experience of the South Commission and its follow-up mechanism, and from recognition of the need to enhance South–South cooperation.

In pursuing its objectives of promoting South solidarity and South–South cooperation, the South Centre provides intellectual and policy support required by developing countries on wide ranging issues, including trade for development, innovation and access to knowledge, climate change and global governance for development.

The centre has three principal organs to achieve the objectives of the South Centre: the Council of Representatives made up of the representatives of the members states; the Board made up of a chairperson and nine members, all highly distinguished individuals from the South, acting in their personal capacity; and the Secretariat, headed by the executive director.

Benjamin W. Mkapa, the immediate former president of Tanzania is the chairperson of the South Centre. The current Board members include Chief Emeka Anyaoku (Nigeria), Norman Girvan (Jamaica), Deepak Nayyar (India), José Antonio Ocampo (Colombia), Zhaoxing Li (China), Leticia Ramos Shahani (Philippines) and Yousef Al Zalzalah (Kuwait).

For detailed information about the South Centre, its activities and publications, visit the website www.southcentre.org (in English, French and Spanish).

Fahamu has a vision of the world where people organise to emancipate themselves from all forms of oppression, recognise their social responsibilities, respect each other's differences, and realise their full potential.

Fahamu supports the strengthening of human rights and social justice movements by:

- promoting innovative use of information and communications technologies
- stimulating debate, discussion and analyses
- publishing news and information
- developing and delivering educational courses, including by distance learning.

Fahamu has offices in Cape Town, Dakar, Nairobi and Oxford.

For more see www.fahamu.org.

 Fahamu Books is a pan-African publisher of progressive books that stimulate debate, discussion and analysis on human rights and social justice in Africa by Africans. Our books are available in many African countries (see list on pp. 142–3) and also in the North. They are also available from our website www.fahamubooks.org.

 Fahamu publishes the prize-winning weekly electronic news and information forum for social justice in Africa, Pambazuka News. It is produced by a pan-African community of some 1,000 citizens and organisations – academics, policy makers, social activists, women's organisations, civil society organisations, writers, artists, poets, bloggers, and commentators.

It is published in English, French and Portuguese.

For more see www.pambazuka.org.

Index

accountability, aid-dependent countries 3

Accra, conference on aid effectiveness (2008) 108, 132

Accra Action Agenda (AAA) 108–15

Afghanistan 20, 31, 72

Africa

    aid trap 129

    booster aid 97–8, 131

    Red Aid 61

    resource gap 91–4

    US aid 31

African, Caribbean and Pacific (ACP) countries, compensatory finance 36–8

African Command (AFRICOM) 31

aid

    0.7 per cent target 1–2, 130–1

    booster theory 97–8, 131

    colour classification 16–18, 131

    conditionalities 20–2, 25–6, 44–5, 61, 106

    dependence 75–7

    and development 128, 130

    false questions and solutions 39–41

    predictability 112–13

    see also official development assistance

aid architecture

    institutions of 105–15, 132

    restructuring 116–25

types of aid 103–5

Aid Effectiveness Reviews (AERs) 112

aid efficiency 97

aid exit strategy

    budgeting for the poor 79–85

    democratic priorities 97–8

    domestic market 88–91

    employment and wages 85–8

    mindset adjustment 77–9, 131–2

    national savings 94–6

    resource gap 91–4

    seven steps 77–98, 131–2

Anglo-American Corporation 119

Angola 31–2, 92

Argentina, Red Aid 60–1

Banco del Sur 121

Blair Commission for Africa 11

booster aid 97–8, 131

Botswana, domestic market 88–9

Brazil

    Partnership Budget Planning 84

    see also BRIC countries

Bretton Woods institutions 105, 116

    see also International Monetary Fund; World Bank

BRIC countries (Brazil, Russia, India and China), and Red Aid 118

budgets

    budget support 111–12

gendered 79
pro poor 82–5
traditional 80–2

Castro, Fidel 83
Chang, Ha-Joon 90
Chiluba, Frederick 46–7
China 23, 88
    see also BRIC countries
civil society
    and Paris Declaration on Aid
    Effectiveness 114–15
    see also non-governmental organ-
    isations (NGOs)
climate change
    and aid 21, 29, 36, 78–9, 113
    World Bank role 120
Cold War 68, 69
commercial aid *see* Orange Aid
Commission on Growth and
Development 15
communities, investments 96
compensatory finance 36–8
concessionary loans
    ODA 5–6, 9
    Orange Aid 25–6
Cuba, people's budget planning 83

DAC *see* Development Assistance
Committee
debt relief, as aid 26–7
developing countries
    development definition 13–14,
    16, 33
    employment 85–8
    independence 66–8, 129
    national project 66–70

Non-Aligned Movement (NAM)
    68, 69–70, 73–5
development
    and aid 128, 130
    definitions 12–16, 128, 130
    endogenous 78–9
    failure of 116–17
    neoliberal definition 14–15
    social democratic model 15–16
    Southern perspective 13–14, 16
    South–South cooperation 33,
    124–5
development aid *see* official development assistance (ODA)
Development Assistance Committee
(DAC)
    accountability of 10
    future of 117–18, 132
    Network on Governance
    (GOVNET) 107
    ODA definition 4–7
    role of 106–7
    Working Party on Aid
    Effectiveness (WPAE) 107, 114
Development Cooperation Forum
(DCF) 115, 122–4, 133
domestic market, creation of 88–91
donor countries
    0.7 per cent pledge 1–2, 130–1
    coherence in ODA use 17–18
    national budget planning 81–2
    Red Aid 23

East Asia, financial crisis (1997–98)
59–60
Easterly, William 19
employment, incomes 85–8

endogenous development 78–9

European Union (EU), and African, Caribbean and Pacific (ACP) countries 36–8

export-led development 90

foreign direct investment (FDI), impact of 9–10, 79

G8 meeting, Gleneagles (2005) 10–11, 26–7

G33 110

G77 70, 73–5, 122–3

gender relations, aid 79

globalisation
and aid dependence 65–6
neoliberalism 71–2

global public goods (GPGs) 34–8, 78–9, 99–100

Green/Blue Aid
definition 18, 34–8, 131
effects of 44
future of 99–100

Group of 77 see G77

Gulf States, domestic market 88–9

Havana Declaration (1979) 70

hearts and minds, Red Aid objective 20, 22–3

IBRD see World Bank

ideological aid see Red Aid

IMF see International Monetary Fund

imperialism, development factor 14

imperial project 19–20, 22, 23–4, 125, 129–30

incomes, inequalities 85–8

independence, national project 66–8, 129–30

India
Citizen's Forum 83–4
see also BRIC countries

Indonesia, financial crisis 59–60

informal sector, employment 87–8

institutions, establishment by Red Aid 23

International Bank for Reconstruction and Development (IBRD) see World Bank

International Centre for Settlement of Investment Disputes (ICSID) 106

International Development Association (IDA) 105

International Finance Corporation (IFC) 105

internationally agreed development goals (IADGs) 115

International Monetary Fund (IMF)
Argentina 60–1
East Asian financial crisis 59
future of 121–2, 132
structural adjustment programmes 45–7, 49–52, 129
and United States 62–3
Zambia structural adjustment 45–7
Zimbabwe structural adjustment 49–52

international non-governmental organisations (INGOs), ODA contributions 6–7

investments, state assets 94–6

Iraq 20, 31, 72

Israel, military aid from US 30–1

Kipling, Rudyard 19
knowledge transfer
      Red Aid 22–3, 24
      South to North 24
Korea, IMF conditionalities 59–60, 62

labour force, incomes 85–8
least developed countries
      employment 86–8
      see also developing countries

Malaysia, financial crisis 59–60
Meltzer Commission 62–3, 121
Mexico, Red Aid 58
military aid
      ODA exclusion 6, 8, 33, 130
      as Yellow Aid 28–34, 99
Millennium Development Goals
(MDGs) 74, 108, 109, 112, 115
mindset, aid dependence 77–9,
131–2
'mission creep' 62, 121
Monterrey Consensus (2001) 80, 107
Morales, Evo 83
Multilateral Investment Guarantee
Agency (MIGA) 105

national project
      definition 4, 66–7
      demise of 71–2
      international dimension 67–9
      national and international
      aspects 69–70
      revival 72–5, 129–30
national savings 94–6
neocolonialism 69
neoliberalism 14–15, 71–2

Network on Governance (GOVNET)
107
Nkrumah, Kwame 69
Non-Aligned Movement (NAM) 68,
69–70, 73–5
non-developmental aid see Orange
Aid
non-governmental organisations
(NGOs)
      aid role 100
      international NGOs (INGOs) 6–7
      participatory planning 81
Nyerere, Mwalimu Julius 13, 16, 128

ODA see official development assist-
ance
OECD see Organisation for
Economic Cooperation and
Development
official development assistance
(ODA)
      coherence in donor countries
      17–18
      concessional loans 5–6, 9
      definitions 4–5, 8, 41, 130
      eligibility criteria 5–7
      problems 7–12
      see also aid
official equity investments (OEIs) 10
oil, prices 72
Orange Aid
      definition 19, 25–8, 131
      future of 99
      illegitimacy as aid 103, 104
Organisation for Economic
Cooperation and Development
(OECD)
      Fragile States Group 107

future of 117–19, 132
ODA definition 4–7, 41
Paris Declaration on Aid
Effectiveness 22, 98, 107–15, 118,
132
role of 106–7
see also Development Assistance
Committee

Panchsheel principles 68
Paris Declaration on Aid
Effectiveness (PDAE) 98, 107–15,
118, 132
participatory planning 81
Philippines, financial crisis 59–60
political aid, as Yellow Aid 28–34,
130
poor, and national budgets 82–5
Poverty Reduction Strategy Papers
(PRSPs) 81
Purple Aid
definition 18, 38–9, 131
empowering effect 44
future of 100
legitimacy as aid 103–4

Red Aid
Africa 61
Argentina 60–1
definition 18–20, 131
donors 23
East Asia 59–60
effects of 44–5
future of 99
illegitimacy as aid 103, 104
imperial factor 19, 22, 23–4, 129
knowledge transfer 22–3, 24
Mexico 58

World Bank 20–2
Zambia 45–7
Zimbabwe 47–57
refugee assistance 27–8
resource gap, Africa 91–4
Rodrik, Dani 120
Russia *see* BRIC countries

Said, Edward 19
Singapore issues 66, 111
social democratic model, develop-
ment definition 15–16
solidarity, Purple Aid 38–9
Somavia, Juan 85, 86
Soros, George 32
South *see* developing countries
South Africa, and donor countries
82
South Centre 123
South–South cooperation 124–5, 133
structural adjustment programmes
Zambia 45–7
Zimbabwe 50–2
Subramanian, Arvind 120
Summers, Larry 62, 63

terrorism, war on 72
Thailand, financial crisis 59–60
Third World *see* developing coun-
tries
Tsvangirai, Morgan 57

United Kingdom, and Zimbabwe
55, 57
United Nations (UN), and Paris
Declaration on Aid Effectiveness
109
United Nations Conference on Trade

and Development (UNCTAD) 66
    Least Developed Country Report
    (2006) 86–8
United Nations Framework
Convention on Climate Change
(UNFCCC) 36, 120
United States
    and IMF 62–3
    military aid to Israel 30–1

Venezuela, Purple Aid 39
village level planning 82–5

Washington consensus 60, 61, 71,
73, 129–30
women, budgeting for 79
Working Party on Aid Effectiveness
(WPAE) 107, 114
World Bank
    Aid Effectiveness Reviews
    (AERs) 112
    future of 120, 132
    Red Aid 20–2, 62–3
    role of 105–6, 110
World Bank Institute 106
World Development Reports 106
World Intellectual Property
Organisation (WIPO) 66
World Trade Organisation (WTO)
    developing countries 66, 111
    Doha round 109–10
    and Paris Declaration on Aid
    Effectiveness 111

Yellow Aid
    definition 19, 28–34, 130, 131
    effects of 44
    future of 99

    legitimacy as aid 103, 104
Zambia, structural adjustment 45–7
Zimbabwe
    and donor countries 82, 119
    financial liberalisation 53–7
    land reform 54–5, 57
    Red Aid 47–57, 130
    structural adjustment pro-
    gramme 50–2

This book is available in the following countries

Botswana
Botswana Book Centre
The Mall, PO Box 91
Gaborone
Botswana
tjiyapo@botsnet.bw
www.bbc.co.bw

Ethiopia
Shama Plc
PO Box 57
Addis Ababa
Ethiopia
Tel: +251 9112013; 00251115545290
shama@ethionet.et

Ghana, Sierra Leone, Benin and Liberia
EPP Books Services
LA Education Cen. PO Box TF490
Trade Fair
Accra
Ghana
Tel: +233 21 778347
Fax: +233 21 779099
gibrine.adam@eppbookservices.com

Namibia
Windhoek Book Den
Shop 19, Gutenberg Platz
Stuebel Street
PO Box 3469
Windhoek
Namibia
Tel: +264 61 239976
Fax: +264 61 234248
elmarie@bookden.com.na

Nigeria
Mosuro
52 Magazine Road
Jericho, POB 30201
Ibadan
Nigeria
Tel: +234 (0)2 241 3375
Fax: +234 (0)2 241 3374
mosuro@skannet.com

Mr Cass Biriyok
Office and Book World Ltd
12 Dock Offices
Surrey Quays Road
London SE16 2XU
Tel: +44 (0)207 3941017
Fax: +44 (0)207 394 8273
info@officeandbookworld.com

Rwanda
Ikirezi Bookshop
Avenue de la Paix
Kigali
Rwanda
Tel +250 571314/570298
info@ikirezi.biz
www.ikirezi.biz

Tanzania
A Novel Idea Bookshop
PO Box 76513
Dar es Salaam
Tanzania
Tel/Fax: +255 (0)22 2601088
www.anovelidea.co.tz

Uganda
Fountain Publishers Ltd
55 Nkrumah Road, PO Box 488
Kampala
Uganda
jtumusiime@fountainpublishers.
co.ug

Zambia
Alabaster Books
Office No 5, Findeco House
PO Box 38264
Lusaka
Zambia
Joesiwo@yahoo.com
Tel: +260 1233258; +2609 77746904

About the author

 Yash Tandon is the executive director of the South Centre, Geneva, an intergovernmental think tank of the developing countries. Professor Tandon's long career in national and international development spans time as a policymaker, a political activist, a professor and a public intellectual. He has written over 100 scholarly articles and has authored and edited books on wide-ranging subjects from African politics to peace and security, trade and the WTO, international economics, South–South cooperation and human rights. He has also served on several advisory committees.

LaVergne, TN USA
15 December 2009
167059LV00002B/1/P